"*This book is a life-chang... ...you won't want to miss. It will make you stop and think and encourage you to be all you can be through Christ. It's moving, inspiring, heart-wrenching, powerful, encouraging, stirring.*"

Barb Long, Washington, IL

Sara's story touched each and every part of me. The thread of writing, the manner and story line flows with such anointing and power. The true meaning of forgiveness was revealed to me, and the encouraging belief that I matter to God. Sara's story is powerful and life-changing.

Robyn Speciale, Peoria, IL

"*This is an amazingly powerful story, triumphant in Christ. It's an awesome example of how all things are possible through Christ Jesus. Powerful, heart-wrenching, eye-opening, amazing.*"

Kimberly Smick, Washington, IL

"*A one-of-a-kind experience; a chance to see that God really will bring beauty from pain. It's profound, comfortable, encouraging, and intimate.*"

Melissa Smith, Washington, IL

Now I Lay Me Down to Sleep

THE STORY OF SARA

"Evil flourishes when good men do nothing" – Edmund Burke 1729–1997

To Laura

Love,
Nena Macon

Now I Lay Me Down to Sleep

THE STORY OF SARA

a true story by

JEN MILLER

TATE PUBLISHING & *Enterprises*

Published by Tate Publishing & Enterprises, LLC
127 E. Trade Center Terrace | Mustang, Oklahoma 73064 USA
1.888.361.9473 | www.tatepublishing.com

Tate Publishing is committed to excellence in the publishing industry. The company reflects the philosophy established by the founders, based on Psalm 68:11,
"The Lord gave the word and great was the company of those who published it."

Book design copyright © 2008 by Tate Publishing, LLC. All rights reserved.
Cover design by Steven Jeffrey
Interior design by Nathan Harmony

Published in the United States of America

ISBN: 978-1-60462-901-9
1. Family & Relationships: Abuse
2. Inspiration: Motivational: Biography & Autobiography
08.07.25

Dedication

To all the little girls, young and aged, who just want to be loved simply because you are you. Who long for true security, value … and hope, in a seemingly hopeless life. There *is* hope—and ALL these things—*for you.*

Acknowledgements

Foremost, *to God*, who is *all* things to me and without whom I would not be, the author and finisher of my faith. Thank you, Abba, for *all* things. To You be all glory, praise, and honor—forever. *I love you*, with all my heart, with all my soul, and with all my mind.

To my husband, Dale, who extends true love to me, without condition. Thank you for always encouraging and supporting my every hope and dream. You are a true knight, in every sense of the word, the one who brings me daisies and pearls. *Thank you.* Thank you for all you have done, and all you have been to me, and our children, through this life journey together. You are my love, my partner, my friend—for always. *I love you.*

To my children, Bobby and Hannah-June, who make me

laugh like no other on this earth. You both fill me with the greatest joy and pride. My love for you dwells in that purest place, deep in my heart, that only a mother can know. I'm very proud of who you are and who you are becoming. You will always be "my babies."

Go with God—no matter what—and embrace this truth: When life seems to have failed you (and it will), "These three remain: faith, hope, and love. But the greatest of these is love" (I Corinthians 13:13). God's love for you, and yours for Him, will never fail. These three things will be your buoy, your shelter, your rock, your manna, your drink. With everything I am, *I love you*, for all eternity.

To my mama, who showed me how to love and persevere. My life motto you inscribed on my heart from an early age, with the permanent ink of a mother's love: *"Where there's a will, there's a way."* You fill my heart to bursting and always have. *I love you*—160*!*

To my sister, Aundi, who—like Jesus—has never left me or forsaken me. Through good and bad, right and wrong, in agreement and disagreement … unconditionally. This thank you is far loftier than human words, and resonates through heaven and earth. What a privilege to be your sister. How blessed I am. Thank you … for all eternity. *I love you.*

To my brothers, Vic, Ira, and Chris (my "Buddy-Pal"), who each sincerely share in my joys, my sorrows, my *life*. Thank you for always being there, for being true brothers. Thank you for your encouragement and support. Thank you for standing strong around me—no matter what. I am proud to be your sister. *All my love and gratitude—for always.*

To John and Eve, a true "brother and sister" to me. Thank you…thank you for standing with me, behind me, beside me…and for giving me a safe place to land and be sheltered at any time, for any reason. You prove unconditional love, and my love is returned to you without measure.

To my dear family-friends, Monnie and Gary, who supports me and loves me without question or expectation. You have covered many a weekend entertaining "Missy" (and being entertained!), to allow me to freely write. Thank you for your committed and selfless love, prayers, encouragements, and avid support. *All my love and gratitude.*

New-made friendships, like new wine,
Age will mellow and refine.

Joseph Parry, 1841–1903,
Welsh composer and musician

To my "Oaks," Amber, Angie, Barb, Debbi, Karen (my angel), Robyn, and Trixie—You have been my protectors, my warriors, my angels on earth, my cheerleaders, my cup bearers…my sisters, and so much more. There are not human words adequate to express my gratitude. Priceless gems will adorn your crowns for your faithfulness to the one, true, and living God. Thank you for surrounding me, and always speaking the truth in love. *I love you with the indescribable love of Christ.*—Your "Daisy"

To my "Warriors," Debbi and Robyn, with whom I share spiritual DNA. Thank you for partnering with me … in so many ways. How proud I am of you for reaching out for your dreams and tightly embracing them, and for remaining faithful to the Spirit in the midst of great adversity. You will be rewarded. I love you for so many reasons … and just because you are you. I count it a privilege to be called your friend, your sister. *I love you.*

To Pat, my true Godsend "for such a time as this." How can I thank you? Adequate words elude me for the time you have graciously invested in me, for the heart you have for ministry, and for seeing and embracing the critical need for this book to reach women, men, and the church. Thank you for cheering me on and standing strong beside me. I am ever indebted and ever grateful. *My love to you.*

Foreword

When the storm came up on the Sea of Galilee, the disciples thought that they were going to die. No, they were sure they were going to die. "Master, don't you care that we are drowning?" they said to Jesus. They had seen storms before, but this one was so big and so furious, beyond their ability to bail and row, and beyond the power of the Lord to help them. Or so they thought.

The book in your hands is the story of a woman who made it through the storm; one of the most furious storms anyone on earth can ever face. Many women who go through storms like this one don't make it. They do die; some of them literally and others of them emotionally, psychologically, spiritually. But the power of Jesus to help is real, though for a long time in their lives it seems like He is asleep in the boat. But Sara knows that He has power to save.

This is a story of unspeakable hardship and cruelty that no young girl anywhere has strength to bear. No adult does either. But God has both the strength and the love that carries her through, and He shares them both in surprising ways.

This is a life-long reclamation story. We have had the joy of knowing Jen, her husband Dale, and their children for many years, and seeing the tender, steady love of God at work. She is one of the sweet agents of grace that God is using today, and we are sure that this story will be a beacon of hope for you.

So read on, and sense the presence and help of God through the storm.

Beth and Pastor Jim Pocock
Wayland, Massachusetts

Though He slay me, yet will I trust in Him.

Job 13:15 (KJV)

Chapter One

"He sealed within her that she was worth nothing, and left her only with the greatest, deepest, all-consuming hatred, and a death sentence."

She was trapped between the bright lights and activity inside the Safeway where she stood, and the imposing night darkness outside the enormous plate glass windows. Her tiny back was pressed into the short, cold wall that anchored the glaring panes rising high above her, as if she were trying to disappear into the mass of concrete. She wanted nothing more than to disappear.

Her intrinsic "fight or flight" dictated that she flee. She wanted to flee, but ... she could do nothing. Fear paralyzed her. She was far too young and powerless to fight him. She was trapped between panic, pushing her to run—run as fast and far away as possible—and the reality of nowhere to flee, no place to hide.[1]

She was only four, far too young to be trapped between love and hatred, good and evil.

Sweating from fear, but shivering from thoughts of her impending punishment, she felt exposed to the world, as if naked. Her only blanket of comfort, and sense of security, was her thick, knee-length hair. It had never been cut since her birth and hung around her petite frame like a shiny, golden shroud, but didn't hide her. It couldn't protect her.

In contrast to the brightness inside the store that commanded over the outer darkness, the ebony blackness of inner fear and the very real presence of evil threatened to consume her.

Her muted whimpering and silent trickle of tears subdued the activity of her younger brother and older sister, impatiently waiting near her for their parents to be finished in the checkout line. They were all tired and ready to go home, and now *this*... they would be forced to hear her screams. Trapped—no place to run, no place to hide. They were trapped between heart-tugging sympathy for her certain fate, anger at her putting them in this position, and relief that it wasn't them in her place... this time.

Not knowing what to do with herself as she quietly cried, but her panic necessitating activity, she unconsciously chewed on the ragged, well-bitten nails of her right hand. Her left hand kept busy tangled in the skirt of her mid-calf, cotton dress. She subtly but incessantly twisted the cool fabric between her damp thumb and forefinger. Her right leg trembled and began to feel numb with recent memories of the same fate that again stood imposing before her like a death trap.

The minutes moved like hours as she watched her daddy pay for the groceries, standing in authority next to her timid mama. He always chatted happily with the young cashiers, like there was never a care in the world, a real-life Jekyll and Hyde.

Why did he not ever chat with her like that, his own daughter? She didn't understand how he could be so cruel to her, just because she had been playing in the aisles with her brother and sister, bored from the endless shopping. These thoughts and questions raced in tandem with images of the punishment he had promised her "when we get home." He'd never change his mind—never! He always did what he said he was going to do to his children ... *always*.

Sara was born into a cult-like and prison-like existence where she was raised until the age of nineteen when she escaped. In our naiveté as children, we didn't recognize that she was living in that kind of environment. We were just children, living within the narrow parameters of a young mind. It wasn't until our early adult years that we realized the magnitude and implications of all she had lived through.

The cult-like existence stemmed from the intensely fundamental church into which Sara and her four siblings were born and raised. Their church was one whose primary salvation message was built on a stone-cold foundation of fear— fear of an ever-burning hell and ghastly eternal suffering for all who did not repent and believe in Jesus, and who did not live by the letter of the laws written by a seemingly unmerciful God. While many of the teachings were, in fact, Biblical truths, there was no love of God emphasized, no manifestation or testifying of the Spirit, no intimate relationship with Jesus Christ, no freedom. There was only law, as interpreted and enforced by "daddy."

Daily, for nineteen years, Sara was inundated with fear: fear of God's—and her daddy's—supreme judgment. She and her siblings walked a tightrope trying to follow the stringent rules he demanded, often in the name of God and His Word. She was taught of a God set apart and unapproachable, powerful and judging, like her daddy. Her and her siblings' life was a prison sentence, their daddy the self-appointed warden.

Sara recalls a time in church, very early in her life—age four. In those days, the early 1960s, there was no such thing as Children's Church. Everyone of all ages sat together on long, hard and cold, wooden pews. The huge rock-and-rafter sanctuary was supported by massive beams high above the cold, concrete floor.

Young children sat with their parents throughout the preaching services, unless misbehaving or nursery age. From an early age, Sara and her siblings were expected to keep still and quiet, held hostage by the threat of absolute punishment. They were to be attentive to the ever-thundering voice of the preacher echoing the wages of sin and death, the gnashing of teeth, and the burning of flesh of all who would surely be cast into the everlasting flames of hell for all of eternity, if they did not repent of their evil, wicked ways and be "saved."

Sara sat terrified, week after week, often crying and clinging to her mama's arm, her tiny body pressed close to her side. Hearing the horrifying rendition of everlasting torture three or more times a week, gripped Sara's young mind and heart. It led her to dwell on thoughts of her mama dying, leaving her alone with her terrorizing, unloving daddy.

Sara loved her mama very, very deeply, contrary to the grave and all-consuming fear and distrust she felt toward her daddy. Her mama and daddy were polar opposites. Her mama was highly affectionate, loving, caring, supportive, encouraging, and fun with her children. Her daddy was none of these things, only fear incarnate. Later in life, Sara would see her mama's qualities as attempt to do everything possible—within the confines of her own fears—to counter the merciless actions of her husband against their children.

"What's the matter?" Her mama would lean down and whisper to Sara as she clung to her side, quietly crying as the preacher shouted. But Sara couldn't put her fears and insecurities into words. She just knew that she was afraid her mama would die and leave her. She thought about this all the time. She didn't understand that she was afraid of losing the only love, affection, and sense of security she had in life. She was far too young to consciously understand, much less articulate, the source of her fears. All she knew was that thoughts of her mama dying gripped her heart, continually—especially each time she sat under the thundering voice of doom resonating through the enormous, cold building called "church."

Sara remembers a night long ago, as clearly as if it were just yesterday.

She was only four-years-old. Her parents left the children with their older cousins, visiting from out of state, for a rare night out to dinner with Sara's aunt and uncle. A heavy storm was raging outside their little duplex on Pine Street as her mama and daddy left for the evening. With each clash of thunder, in tempo with howling winds and pounding rain, Sara cried with terror and grief that her mama wouldn't come back home to her. Even at that young age she had no allegiance, no concern or care, for her daddy. He had already severed any ties of love or compassion that a young girl would naturally feel toward her daddy.

❤ ❤ ❤

Near Sara's fifth birthday, the family moved from the small duplex into their very own house, equally small. Moving to a new place felt exciting to Sara as she mirrored her parent's joy. It was as if, by moving, everything would suddenly be new and different—better. But her anticipation and hopes were soon dashed when Sara overheard her parents talking with the widower about why he was selling the fairly new house on Meadow Lane, leaving an evil omen hanging in the air. Like any interested buyers, her parents wanted to know why the man was selling his house, assurance that nothing was wrong with their potential first investment.

"My wife…" the older man hesitated, somber, "she died … drowned in the bathtub."

The horror! Images of a dead woman, lying submerged in *their* new bathtub, her blue and puffy face staring wide-eyed toward the ceiling, were seared into Sara's mind—forever.

Looking back, Sara could believe that the drowning of the woman was indeed an omen of the evil that house would contain over the next fourteen years. The images of a dead woman floating in the bathtub replayed in Sara's mind every time she took a bath. Her mind conjured fears of dying by drowning. She would carry these images and fears into adulthood, perpetuating the phobia she would gain—"hydrophobia." Later in life, water related accidents would further cement this irrational terror in her. Even today, Sara thinks of drowning each time she drives her car across a bridge, over a body of water, and whenever she is near a lake, a swimming pool, the ocean.

Chapter Two

Sara's home life was ruled by her daddy—an iron-fisted man of strong, stern will and no outward love, a man possessed and obsessed, a man whose abusive discipline of his children was ritualistic and sadistic, and whose practices of religion were intermixed with his practices of the satanic spiritual world.

Other than church-related activities, Sara and her siblings were allowed very little existence outside their house for fourteen years. She was never allowed to participate in any school activities, only attending classes. As an early elementary student, Sara was not even allowed to participate in music during class time. Her daddy saw secularism of any kind as wrong, except where it pertained to his own desires. As you can imagine, it was highly embarrassing and shaming, as a young child, to be ostracized—made to sit apart and alone from her classmates as they all participated in music. This alienation fed Sara's growing feelings of worthlessness and insecurity.

Throughout her twelve years in public schools, Sara was never allowed to participate in any school activities. No sporting events. Certainly no dances—dancing was a sin. No senior prom. She was only allowed to attend classes and church-related activities.

Sara never saw the inside of a movie theater in all her years living at home. It was a rare and immensely exciting opportunity when she and her sister, Alexandria (Allie), were allowed to spend the night with a girlfriend from church, go home with a friend after the Sunday morning service, or when a friend got to come home with them. Otherwise, Sara's existence was isolated to their tiny, two-bedroom house of horrors, shared by seven people.

All five children shared one bedroom, just large enough for two twin beds, separated by a small lamp table, a set of bunk beds, an ancient roll-out bed, and a homemade vanity that her daddy had handcrafted. Sara's parents shared the other bedroom, three feet across the narrow hallway.

Around the time she and Allie were preteens, they gained the set of twin beds from a relative. Sara's bed was the one pinned into the corner walls, with a window along its length. She would often lay and stare up at the stars and the moon. The serenity of nature never failed to bring her peace and hope. She slept in that bed throughout the dark, oppressive years, only the wall hugging her in the night, only the stars and moon her friend, her comfort. Her bed was the only space she could truly call her own, but even that space would be stolen, invaded, and defiled by sin, terror, and evil.

♥ ♥ ♥

In stark contrast to Sara's daddy, her mama was very attentive to her young children. She would read to them, snuggle
and take naps with them. She would often tell them that
she loved them "sixty." This seemed like an enormous number to their young minds. As they grew older, they'd one-up
her with "sixty-one," or "sixty-nine." She'd make games of
the chores they were assigned. The stainless steel flatware
became soldiers that Sara and Allie put to bed as they dried
the freshly washed utensils standing in the plastic dishd-
rainer. Her mama would find every opportunity to act silly
to keep them laughing, and often found *something* in their
otherwise oppressive life to bring such uncontrollable laughter from herself that she would segue into crying. Sara found
this to be an intriguing phenomenon, that her mama could
laugh so hard she'd end up sobbing.

Every night when the children went to bed, Sara's mama
would tuck them in, give them kisses, and tell them she
loved them. Then she'd lead them in the common children's
prayer we've all heard, but perhaps with a little different
twist depending on where in the U.S. you were raised. Sara
learned it like this, "Now I lay me down to sleep. I pray the
Lord my soul to keep. If I should die before I wake, I pray
the Lord my soul to take."

Sara and her siblings were subject to harsh disciplines
and grossly abusive punishments by their daddy—all too
staggering for a person of any age, much less a young, tender
child. Sara lived in constant fear of harm and even death.

The punishment in Sara's house for every wrong doing,

no matter the degree, was the same. If one talked back, didn't get a chore done, didn't finish all the food on their plate, talked in church or ran in church, failed to get good grades, got too loud or cried too long… every offense was met with the same punishment. Sara was made to pull down her panties, bend over her daddy's bed with the shame of her nakedness exposed to him, and he would repeatedly whip her with his leather belt, using his full strength. Sara was whipped a lot. Her oldest brother, Matt, fifteen months younger, was the proverbial "black sheep" and also the object of their daddy's wrath. There were times when her daddy whipped Matt mercilessly and Sara thought he would literally beat Matt to death. The screams and pleadings of his cries were unbearable to Sara and her other siblings.

To be placed in a position completely without power, and unable to shut out the screaming and begging of someone you love, so young and helpless being beaten, wreaks havoc in your mind, in your emotions, and in your body. Your blood runs cold and a hot surge of all-consuming hatred swells inside your head and pushes through your chest, constricting your breathing. The sheer injustice rages through you and the power of adrenaline rushes down through your arms, your stomach, and your legs, causing your muscles to harden in restraint against the natural urge to retaliate. You begin to shake uncontrollably out of immense fear, fury, hatred, and helplessness. In that moment, you know that you could kill another person to save the one you love from the awful pain they're enduring at the relentless hands of a monster. No child, no adult, was ever meant to experience such cruelty. Sara did—again and again—for many years.

Ephesians 6:4 says, "Fathers, do not provoke your children to wrath." God had a good reason for including this commandment in His Word.

Whipping in Sara's house was a methodical, merciless procedure. It was as though some other being would take over her daddy's mind and body in the process, stripping him of feeling, compassion, and human kindness. Looking into his eyes often gave Sara the sense that her daddy was not there, that something else, something evil, was looking back at her. It was very unnerving and unsettling to see the eyes of another presence looking at her through her daddy's eyes.

Sara never spoke of this to anyone, though one time a friend stated to her, unprompted, that her daddy's eyes looked weird and scared her. This admission was affirming for Sara, that she was not imagining what she was seeing. There was something sinister and "other-worldly" that peered through his eyes, seemingly apart from him, yet owning him … and had taken up residence in his body.

Scripture tells us that our eyes are reflective of who we truly are on the inside—in our heart. "Your eye is the lamp of your body. When your eyes are good, your whole body also is full of light. But when they are bad, your body also is full of darkness. See to it, then, that the light within you is not darkness" (Luke 11:34–35).

Sara's daddy was a strict, religious fundamentalist to the core, skewing Biblical truths to justify his cruel and heartless behaviors toward his children and their mama. His interpretation of the Proverbs 13:24 and 23:13 exegesis, spare the rod; spoil the child, was full warrant to barbarically whip Sara and Matt.

This is not what God intended by these scriptures. He

does not honor abuse of any kind against His creation. He does not honor abuse of people, young or old: "Do to others as you would have them do to you" (Luke 6:31). He does not honor abuse of His creatures: "Then the Lord opened the donkey's mouth, and she said to Balaam, 'What have I done to you to make you beat me these three times?'" (Numbers 22:28). God does not honor abuse.

"Do not be proud...Do not be conceited" (Romans 12:16), was defined by her daddy as never speaking nor acknowledging the good things his children did or accomplished. The children learned they were not to take pride in anything, lest they be admonished. The *whole* truths of God's Word also includes wholesome, justified, encouraging, uplifting, and motivating pride in addition to admonishing and warning against arrogant, conceited pride. There is a stark and undeniable difference (Proverbs 17:6, Isaiah 4:2, Isaiah 60:50, 2 Corithians 5:12, 2 Corithians 7:4, 2 Corithians 8:24, Galatians 6:4, James 1:9).

How often has a young child, perhaps your own, run to you, their little face beaming up toward yours and thrust a picture into your hand that they'd colored or made "just for you?" Hungry little souls anticipating the filling food of acceptance and thirst-quenching drink of approval that would satisfy, fuel, and nurture their young spirits and spur them toward greater and nobler things.

Most of us would naturally respond with something like, "Oh, honey...that's beautiful! What a good job you did! I'm so proud of you!" Then their little feet would scamper off, all satisfied and happy, secure in knowing they are loved and appreciated, and that their contributions to the world, however small, are valued worthy simply because they are who they are. Never from Sara's daddy.

Children whose positive behaviors and best efforts are not acknowledged and affirmed, grow to be adults who are perfectionists—never satisfied with their utmost efforts, always hungry and never full.

Ever in contrast, Sara's mama consistently told her children she was proud of them. She'd exclaim over their creations, smother their little cheeks with kisses, and wrap their tiny bodies in her arms. She'd tell them often, "You can do anything you set your mind to." Her favorite was, "Where there's a will, there's a way." She quoted this often and in a vast number of circumstances, whether encouraging the children to pick up toys or mow the lawn, to career choices and life dreams. Despite her best efforts, it was critically not enough against the constant threat of trauma and oppression generated by Sara's daddy. Consequently, little Sara grew more and more hungry for love, affection, attention, appreciation, value, and worth. She was not taught that God valued her as His unique creation whom He loved without condition.

> Little girls need their daddy's love. Girls who do not get from their daddies the love, security, and value that God entrusted their daddies to give, will seek out all of these things when they are young women, in any place and in any form they can get it.

Chapter Three

Sara's daddy was a man of gross extremes and little balance. Whether it was creating a new project, preparing a huge, Saturday morning breakfast, repairing a vehicle, planting a garden, participating in church activities, punishing his children … most things were rabid and exaggerated.

To his credit, her daddy enjoyed cooking for the family. Preparations for a typical Saturday morning breakfast would begin as early as 7:00 a.m. with grandiose plans. Eventually, the family could gather around the table, midmorning—starving. There'd be the usual sausage patties, bacon or ham, sometimes in company with pork chops. Fried potatoes, fried eggs, home-made biscuits and sausage gravy would complete the feast.

Even their corner lot among the tract housing became extravagant to city farming, yielding an abundance of fresh fruits and vegetables. Five pecan trees, representing each of the children, lined the length of the yard parallel to the side street that intersected with theirs. Peach, apple, and crabapple trees blossomed each spring and bore summer fruits under their daddy's care. A good measure of the back yard, sharing ground with the fruit trees, was a large garden supplying corn, tomatoes, green onions, radishes, okra, peas, and other assorted vegetables. To flavor, he grew a variety of herbs in beds hugging the back length of the matchbox house. Sara's daddy loved food, but it was challenging to feed a family of seven on his modest income. The garden supplied hearty vetetables, but—like every other venture he adopted—it became grossly disproportionate to the norm.

The children's summer days would often be filled with the overwhelming, looming task of weeding the vegetable garden. Their daddy would instruct that they complete the task by the time he arrived home from work in the evening, or be punished. It was always the same—an unsparing beating. Arguments and disgruntled attitudes would warrant the same.

The weeding was often too monumental an expectation that stretched through the morning and into the heat of the afternoon sun. Should they succeed, there would be no praise, no rewards, no accolades. Should they fail, the balmy, evening dusk would echo with their screams and pleadings as he scourged their bare bottoms with his belt.

Two large geese had run of the chain linked fenced yard. Heckle and Jeckle would squawk at the imposing antics of the young children, teasing, running, and playing around them. In retaliation, the geese would nip and snap at their dress tails and ankles. Squealing with delight, the children would race about the yard, geese at heel. Heckle and Jeckle brought laughter and adventure. The children grew to love their wild and wily pets whose stretched necks made them nearly as tall as the children.

It was disturbingly tragic and traumatic when their daddy announced that Heckle and Jeckel would be butchered, and soon sitting dressed in the center of their supper table. In horror, they begged and cried for him to spare their beloved pets, but to no avail. A new element of death and fear joined hands with Sara's daily thoughts of drowning.

The prevailing stench of anguish hung thick through the days, months, and years of Sara's childhood, ever dancing, spooky shadows on the walls of her mind, fueling her nightmares.

Throughout Sara's childhood, her daddy would call the family together every night, with rare exception, just before bed, for what he hailed as "Daily Bible Readings." It didn't matter if the family had just gotten home at 10:00 p.m. from the midweek preaching service and the children needed to be in bed. The family had "Daily Bible Readings" no matter how late—*every* night.

"Daily Bible Readings" weren't a scripture or two as devotion or food for thought. More often than not, it wasn't simply a chapter or two. Sara's daddy read and read, monotonous chapter after chapter, until *he* grew tried and decided he was done for the night. He had no regard, whatsoever, for the practical wellbeing of his children when it came to sleep. None.

Young children, even older children, are not often physically able to stay awake at a late hour. Their young and rapidly growing bodies need sleep. Naturally, Sara and her siblings would begin to nod off from the endless droning as they sat on the hardwood floor of their living room. Their daddy always sat in *his* chair like a king reigning over his subjects. Whenever one of the children began to nod off, her daddy would command the child to stand. This is how he or she would have to remain throughout the rest of the reading, no matter how long. Any complaints would most assuredly result in a whipping.

Sara dreaded "Daily Bible Readings" and having to sit there for so long, trying so hard to stay awake while he droned on without regard to their physical needs. She knew the dread of being made to stand while he read, and being so tired she couldn't stay awake, and the fear of being whipped if she complained and angered him.

Often times, Sara saw her daddy's endless reading as deliberate, especially when one of the children was made to stand. The injustice of his calculated cruelty burned hot rage within her. She saw on his face, far too often, the perverse pleasure he took in his children's suffering. When punishing his children, she saw the prideful puffiness of power that he wore on his countenance like the robe of a judge. Whether making them stand for long periods late at night, sitting for hours at the supper table until every bite had been eaten from their plates, or watching them pull down their underwear with pleading and panic on their faces when he was going to punish them, he seemed to relish their misery.

She hated him with a searing fury so strong that the

physical restraint against the urge to pummel him felt like the straining of wild dogs held back from ready prey. The hot rage of injustice burned inside her. She wanted to kill him— race across the room to where he sat with that subtle, sick smirk pulling at his mouth and stab his flesh again and again, then rip his skin off strip by strip! Sara feared and despised him to the point of wishing him dead.

♥ ♥ ♥

One week out of every year, he traveled up to Chicago to attend classes for his job. For the children and their mama, it was like a temporary parole from prison. As soon as he stepped on the plane, out of their sight, it was as though a dark and heavy veil timidly lifted from the air, their shoulders, hearts, and minds. It was always the most joyful, freeing week of laughter, peace, and renewed promise that would all too quickly end when he stepped back off the plane six days later.

Intermixed with the joy and laughter was the thorny rope of dread and defeat, knowing their freedom was short-lived. Sara would pray desperately, pleadingly, again and again through the week that his plane would crash and he would die and never come home to them.

"Please, please, don't let him come home," she'd beg ardently to God. But he always came home, and the cruel reality of her life encased her like a closing coffin.

Chapter Four

The family was always together, held under thumb by the commanding control of their daddy except during school hours and church classes. They were at home together every night and on weekends. They grocery shopped together and attended church together three or more times a week. Rarely were the children allowed to be apart from their daddy or mama. They lived a very limited existence from secular society. Rarely could they afford to go out to eat, but when they did, there was a tenuous peak of joy, in hand with a guardedly lighter air, always tempered with towing the line. Children were to be seen and not heard for the most part.

There were many times when either Sara or Matt would inevitably get into trouble and suffer the anquish of facing a beating at the inhumane hands of their daddy. He never, ever forgot when he said he was going to whip them, nor did he ever change his mind.

Sara was nine when one Wednesday evening, following the preaching service, she was playing with her friends and ran across the church foyer. Her daddy saw this and approached her. Seeing his approach, with stern disapproval etched on his face, her stomach turned, knowing her fate. He told her in his quiet and calm but authoritative way that when they got home he was going to teach her never to run in the church again.

Sara's blood ran cold with fear, for she knew well what this meant. She'd been in that place of punishment at the barbarous hands of her daddy many times before. She knew exactly what to expect, or so she thought, based on all the other times she had been beaten, and shamed by her nakedness. She knew he would never change his mind or forget. Her fate was sealed.

Over the next hour, the fear and panic hammered inside her. It made her stomach ill and her chest constrict, hindering her ability to breathe, thinking about her doom. The familiar prickling sensation began to crawl across her bottom and down the back of her legs that would mount to a feverish sensation. She would learn much later, as an adult, that she was experiencing what is termed by the mental health field as a "body memory," a physical reaction caused by conditioned physical trauma.[2]

When Sara's family arrived home that night, her daddy told her to go to his room. She could barely walk as the fear overtook her and constrained her limbs. Hot tears stung her eyes, panic wrenched her heart, and bile rose to her throat as she watched him ceremoniously unbuckle his leather belt and whip it out of his belt loops as he said, "I'm going to teach you not to run in God's house. Pull your panties down and bend over the bed," he commanded. Weeping and pleading, she knew her fate would be even worse if she didn't obey.

It was always the same, every time he'd whip her. He'd make a production of unbuckling his belt as he watched her, hesitant to pull down her panties, shaking with fear and pleading in her eyes. He was always unnaturally calm in the process, like he wasn't really there—like something alien had taken over his body. He always had a look of subtle pleasure about his face. Something demonic stared out from his eyes, a true madman. He was, in fact, a madman, possessed by evil and perhaps unconsciously fueled by the damage done to him in his own childhood.

With all his fury, he lashed the belt across her tender, young flesh again and again. Her screams of pain and begging him to stop, as she tried to shield herself against the blows, reverberated through the small house. The other children—and her mama as well—clutched their ears and buried their heads in a feeble attempt to block out her primal outcries that ravaged their emotions. They wished it was them in her place and thankful it wasn't, a furious dichotomy of the mind.

"Now run down the hallway and back," he commanded. "I'm going to teach you to never run in the church again." Hesitating and sobbing, unable to comprehend the cruelty of his methodical demands, she pleaded and begged and cried, clutching her searing, naked bottom.

"Run down the hallway and back," he demanded again. She had no choice but to obey if she wanted to survive at all.

She ran down the short hallway of their tiny house and back into his room.

"Bend over the bed!" He lashed her again and again against the sounds of her pleading screams. Then he repeated his command for her to run down the hallway and back, and continued to scourge her. Each new thrash felt like razors cutting into her delicate flesh.

Sara doesn't remember how long that particular incident lasted, only that there were many like punishments through the years. And once the punishment ended, she wasn't allowed to cry for long, or she'd be beaten for that as well. She learned to suck it up, push down the tears, the hatred, the pain, the anger, and the injustice festering inside her. She learned to condition herself against any unmanageable, outward displays of emotion that might prompt further physical harm against her. Hatred of him consumed her and flooded her essence with rage.

Whenever he was whipping one of the children, Sara's mama would be crying in the kitchen or the bathroom, too timid to stand up to him and rescue her child from his brutality.

As a young child, did you ever see or hear the parent you love, crying? It creates chaos inside a child's mind and spirit. Seeing her mama crying just heaped on more pain and anger and feelings of injustice inside Sara that she had to stuff down.

Sara learned to feel very deeply for her mama, seeing her almost like another sibling, sharing equal fear and powerlessness against the one who ruled by terror. She didn't know at that young age that it was the critical responsibility and justified action of a parent to step in and stop abuse. She just knew her mama to be attentive, affectionate, caring, gentle, and fun … almost to an extreme, and to feel powerless to protect her babies. He ruled her with an iron fist and keen manipulation, just as he ruled his children.

It wasn't until Sara grew up and became a mama herself that she felt how inconceivable it was that her own mama had not protected her children. She experienced first hand how deeply a mother's love and protection runs for her child. She knew how deeply her own mama loved her, but often asked herself, *why did she not protect me?! Why didn't she stop him?!*

She couldn't imagine *not* protecting her own children from harm threatened or inflicted by another person—no matter who it was. It just didn't make sense in Sara's mind how her mama did not protect her and her siblings. It has never made sense; it's inconceivable. She tried again and again to put herself in her mama's shoes, living in an earlier generation where abuse was not discussed, nor family business, and where it was more accepted that men had the upper hand of authority over their wives and children. While she can understand that it was more difficult in that generation to take a stand against abuse, it was nevertheless a responsibility and the just thing to do.

Sara struggled with the realization of how deeply her mama must have feared and felt intimidated by her husband to be rendered completely paralyzed against the immensely powerful, natural instinct to rise up and protect her babies from harm. But even then, on a gut level, she could not understand her mama's decisions to allow such violence against her children.

Their fundamentalist religion didn't help, but rather negligently encouraged the allowance for abuse of authority and far too often still does today. Sara's daddy skewed the translation of spare the rod; spoil the child, expounded through Proverbs 23, giving license and justification for his heinous misdeeds and perverse pleasures at his children's expense.

♥ ♥ ♥

Sara recalls a night in her elementary years when she and Allie shared the top bunk of beds that were butted into a corner of the small bedroom, before the twin beds came along. The sturdy, imposing structure encroached on a quarter of their small bedroom. Allie slept at the head and Sara at the foot. Her two younger brothers, Matt and John, shared the lower bunk, before Wayne was born.

It was late, after "Daily Bible Readings," and Sara was too warm to get under the covers. Her mama came in to kiss them goodnight and suggested that she cover up. Sara resisted the prompt. Hearing this, her daddy came into the room and commanded her to get under the covers. It didn't matter the temperature in the room; it didn't matter how Sara felt. It was totally a matter of power and control for her daddy.

Sara made the mistake of telling him she was too hot to get under the covers. As a young child, she still had the innocent immaturity to stand up to him without first considering the consequences. Often her fortitude was fueled by the raging fire of anger and resentment burning inside her—like spouts of steam bursting from a pressure cooker.

Her daddy would not be disobeyed and certainly not argued with by his children. Sara was beaten severely that night, then made to swelter under her covers through the night. The burning heat of her hatred, in tandem with the heat of her singeing bottom and legs, and her hands and arms where she had tried to shield herself, made the night all the more stifling and miserable. She wished him dead.

♥ ♥ ♥

Sara had three recurring nightmares throughout her childhood. One was about her brother, Matt, who often suffered as she did. Their daddy treated him ruthlessly, unlike his other two boys. She dreamed again and again that she saw her daddy holding three-year-old Matt upside down by his ankles, over the open toilet, and threatening to dunk his head down under the water.

She could hear the terrified cries of her helpless, young brother ringing endlessly through her mind. Strangely, with each recurrence of the dream, she recalls that the dream was related to Matt's hair being combed with one of those short, black, generic combs. Perhaps Matt had been protesting getting his hair combed, which inexcusably spurred their daddy's anger toward this vile act.

Sara watched the horror of this vision play out again and again in her dreams, to the point of considering—as an adult—that it may not have simply been a nightmare, but rather a reality. Perhaps to her seven-year-old mind it had been *too* frightening to consciously accept and process as reality at the time.

♥ ♥ ♥

Sara never knew from moment to moment what would warrant the next beating. She lived in constant fear of physical harm, constant walking on egg shells, constant "fight or flight." As a result, Sara grew to be from a very early age an extremely nervous child. It wouldn't take much to cause her to cry or be intimidated by her peers. At school, she was terribly shy and self-conscious, bearing little self-worth. She was embarrassed by her hand-me-down clothes, her red plaid, tin lunchbox, and the simple items packed for lunch—though lovingly by her mama. She had become so self-conscious and insecure by junior high that she would go into the bathroom at lunchtime and lock herself in a stall to eat. As disgusting as she thought this was, and would certainly appear to others, she just couldn't face her peers at the lunch tables in the loud and imposing cafeteria.

She was easily intimidated, frightened, and sick to her stomach. When the occasional bully chose to pick on her, she'd be reduced to tears and feel terribly ashamed and humiliated in the face of her peers. She was easy prey for bullies.

All adults intimidated Sara, too—especially men.

There were no adults in Sara's life who were ever attentive or caring enough to take action against the abuse she was under at home. Adults, who *had* noticed, never intervened, as they well should have—not even those relatives who spent consistent time with her family. In that generation, most everyone conducted their own, private lives, raised their children as they saw fit, and certainly didn't share their perverted secrets or seek help to overcome them—like physically and sexually abusing children. There was no open talk of abuse or suspected abuse, not even by clergy, pastors, Sunday school teachers, schoolteachers, or club leaders. Abuse was not publicly defined; nor was public action taken against it—certainly not by any of the adults in Sara's life. Not even relatives or the parents of her closest friends from church stepped in. There were those who looked upon her with pity, knowing how unrelenting her daddy was. Sara saw on their compassionate faces the mixed emotions that clearly said, "It makes me terribly sad and angry that you have such a difficult life." But not one person mustered the courage to intervene. Tragic. Inexcusable.

It was a rare adult who took the time to even befriend a child, much less defend. The consensus of parenting at that time seemed to reflect what her daddy declared to his children with impatience. "Children are to be seen and not heard."

Adults represented one thing to Sara: stern, staunch authority—period. Whenever Sara got into trouble at school for simple things like not focusing on her work or playing around, she also paid the price at home as soon as her daddy found out. Somehow, he always found out. Somehow, her daddy was always privy to Sara's every move and took every excuse to unleash his pleasure in wrath upon her.

Simple misbehaviors or neglected schoolwork in the classroom were both due in large to Sara's inability to focus—a direct result of the constant trauma and abuse at home. Sara was a terribly shy and nervous child who barely peeped a sound in class, much less caused any serious trouble warranting communication with her parents. Nevertheless, the teachers regularly shared with her mama and daddy her slight misconducts and lack of focus with ignorant or negligent disregard for how she would, in turn, be punished at home.

There were signs of abuse that Sara's teachers should have recognized and taken action against, rather than contributing. They should have stepped in and reported the abuse to the authorities. It was simply *wrong* to consciously ignore warnings and signs of abuse and choose to remain uninvolved at the expense of the safety and well-being of a child. It was ethically wrong and unjust.

Chapter Five

Sara was a mere two-year-old when she was made to sing her first solo in church, in front of their large congregation. For many years after, she would be terrified and physically ill each time she was made to perform, or even simply stand with the choir or instrumentalists on stage. She was easily sick to her stomach and quick to vomit from the constant strain of anxiety, intimidation, and fear she lived under.

Music played a huge and intricate part in her home and church life, insisted upon and influenced by her daddy. He was intensely focused in music and art, but music was the higher priority for him. He had a nice tenor voice that he often used in church and with Barbershop quartets through the years. He dabbled with the harmonica and violin and became fairly skilled at both.

He whistled and sang incessantly as he worked—at home, on the job, in the car—everywhere. Sara grew to hate the sound of implied *joy* emanating from his smug lips as if he had no care in the world and all was right and just. The twisted dichotomy between this pretense and the reality of her life sickened her. She despised him and his whistling and singing all the more.

Like everything else about him, the sounds of his whistling and singing made her skin crawl. She'd grow instantly angered and the familiar urge to rise up and physically strike him would quickly seize her. She'd be compelled to scream at him, "Stop! Stop! Stop!" But she didn't dare. In contrast, she'd want to run far away from the sickening sounds—and the pretentious monster.

Still, by default, music became a major part of Sara's life as well. She could have despised it, simply because her daddy lived and moved in it, but she didn't. She only despised some of his preferential and hypocritical use of it. His incessant whistling and singing implied peace and "all is well with the world." The hymns, she would later associate with him and their legalistic church. The down-and-out country tunes wailing from his radio were contrary to the stand he took against secular music when he had prevented her from participating in music during elementary school. There were many double standards that would become increasingly evident to Sara and her siblings through the years.

Music, by nature, is a language without human ownership, bearing mystery and power that only God can claim, one of His greatest creations and gifts to mankind. Despite the purity of music interwoven with the perversive circumstances of her life, God amazingly fulfilled in her His promise from Romans 8:28, "In all things God works for the good of those who love him." Sara grew to love music to a passion.

Her daddy propelled her into the mysterious and awakening world of music from infancy, but it was God alone who divinely nurtured within her the deep and abiding love for music that she would embrace the rest of her life.

Sara and Allie began piano lessons in the first grade. She would grow in awe and deep respect of those God had gifted to create ageless masterpieces of ancient and contemporary works. Having little money and always struggling to make ends meet, piano lessons were a luxury, but one her daddy insisted upon because music was such a high priority to him. The girls never missed their weekly piano lessons in the twelve years they took, except for illness or a rare family vacation. For consistent piano education, she would be grateful.

With piano lessons came recitals. With each recital, Sara grew more and more physically ill from the anxiety and fear of being on stage, in the spotlight and focus of attention. She always felt so exposed, so self-conscious, so intimidated. Being with a group on stage—rather than alone—had no bearing and held no comfort either. Simply sitting among a group of fellow students on stage, she was increasingly anxious and physically ill, even more so when it was her turn to perform.

Annual recital performances typically began with the earliest level students and progressed to the seasoned students performing at the highest levels. The more advanced she became, the longer she would have to sit on stage and wait, feeling increasingly exposed and vulnerable. With each passing minute, she would grow more and more nauseated and stiff with the cold of fear that permeated her body.

Perpetual thoughts of all eyes and ears focused on her and judging her abilities at the piano consumed her mind and fed her stage fright to phobic proportions. Topophobia—stage fright—was added to her exaggerated fear of drowning and thoughts of death. Nevertheless, despite her distress and throwing up at every performance occasion, her daddy would not allow her to miss a recital. It was expected, regardless of how she felt or how it affected her. Condemnation was reality, the fear that taught her to be silent in her suffering.

One Sunday afternoon in late spring, as Sara sat on stage as a teenager having earned advanced placement in the lineup of performers, each passing minute brought her closer to panic and emesis. Her throat began to close up tighter with each ticking second, together with her lungs, impeding her intake of air. It was as though her lungs became paralyzed and would no longer work involuntarily. She juggled conscious reminders to take a breath with working to prevent bile from rising in her throat and the gross embarassment of vomiting on stage.

She could only manage shallow intakes of air, she was so constricted with fear, drawing her like a powerful vacuum toward *hypo*ventilation. The tighter her throat closed and the more the bile from her stomach gagged her, the more she'd have the urge to swallow and the inability to take a breath. It was a vicious cycle too powerful for her to conquer. She felt as though she had no control of her body.

Desperate thoughts that she would vomit, right there on stage, waged war with the embarrasment she'd have by drawing attention to herself if she were to get up and leave the stage. Both options terrified her, perpetuating the panic cycle further and immobilizing her body from moving out of her seat and getting to a toilet, or outside, to throw up.

Before long, she began to openly gag. Certain that all eyes were on her, she sat frozen in her seat. She covered her mouth inconspicuously with the printed program grasped tightly in her cold but sweating hand and continued to fight the gagging and her effort to breathe. It soon overtook her though, and she threw up right there at her seat—on stage. The horror! The humiliation!

Mortified, she felt as though she were walking under water as she made her way off stage to collect herself. Knowing she would have to re-enter again—to perform her piece—she wanted to die! Her hands and fingers stiff with cold, she performed as best as she could when it was her turn—as she did every year—but it was emotional and physical upheaval every time.

Similar experiences accompanied her singing on stage as a teen throughout junior high and high school. She and Allie were an active part of their teen choir at church. It was bad enough just being on stage performing with the choir—which made her ill—but she was also appointed as the designated soloist for several years. She would be sick from anxiety for *days* prior to a performance and nearly immobile as the hour and the moment grew near when she would have to step out in front of the mic and sing—alone.

Panicked anxiety wasn't limited to stage fright. Whenever Sara knew she was facing confrontation or the reprimands of an authority figure, male or female, her body would move through all the familiar physiological stages that would lead to her eventual vomiting, lack of oxygen, and often diarrhea. This was a continuum through her life from an early age, not associated solely with fear, but also with anticipation and excitement as well. Whenever Sara was allowed to attend an extraordinary church youth group activity, like going to Six Flags, or even the rare occasion to sleep over at a church friend's house, the thrill would induce the same psychological process, ending with her throwing up. She was simply unremittingly nervous, conditioned by constant fear and trauma.

Her daddy got highly irritated over her vomiting everytime she got nervous or excited about an activity or event, and would often harshly reprimand her for it. He'd threaten to not allow her to go on the trip with her youth group—or whatever the activity at the time, "If you don't straighten up!" It was a vicious cycle that he himself had created against her. It was as if he had forced her into a washing machine, closed the lid and set the machine on the spin cycle, then blamed *her* for the natural reaction of getting sick. It was absurd! Nonetheless, it was the life in which she was trapped and at his mercy. The rage of injustice coursed through her in silence.

♥ ♥ ♥

From early in her life and throughout much of her early adulthood, Sara's constant fear and nervousness caused her to adopt a growing number of physical and emotional complications. In addition to easily vomiting, and suffering from terribly painful stomach cramps and diarrhea, the worst *visible* sign of her nervousness was the degree to which she bit her fingernails.

Sara couldn't remember a time through her childhood when she did not bite her nails. It wasn't until she was middle age, looking back on her life, that she realized how the abuses must have begun very early in her life for her to have had such great anxiety, fear, and hatred of her daddy from such a young age. It had begun at her birth—in the crib. Her mama had admitted to her how her first "spanking" had been in the crib, because she wouldn't stop crying. She had been birthed into abuse.

She bit her nails so badly that they would bleed and become puffy with infection, but she couldn't stop. Biting her nails was an outward cry for help that mimicked physically the constant fear and trauma always churning inside her little body.

Her daddy hated this habit. He saw Sara's nail-biting as a form of disobedience because he had demanded she stop, but she didn't—she *couldn't*. He was not to be disobeyed, though. He had to have control over every area of her existence, and was determined to make her stop that habit.

She bit her fingernails because of the impossible expectations and fear consuming her young mind, a natural stress-relieving tool, and an outward sign of anxiety. The more he tried to make her stop, the more she was inherently driven to bite her nails, another vicious cycle for little Sara.

He tried the tactic of shame and humiliation to get her to quit biting her nails, by forcing her to wear her little, white kid gloves all the time, even to school. It wasn't so bad wearing them to church because it was quite common in the south to "dress up" for church and not uncommon for little girls to don their white kid gloves. Wearing them to school was altogether a different story. It was humiliating and drew demoralizing attention from the other children. Sara would cry with shame and embarrassment at being made to wear her gloves to school every day. And the gloves were hot and sweaty, adding to her misery. And she was expected to perform well in her studies at school?! The mounting pressure he imposed on her to stop biting her nails just caused her to continue biting.

Naturally, she had to remove the gloves to wash her hands, eat, and bathe, so this method to eliminate her habit didn't work for him either. When the gloves came off, she bit her nails. This led him to wrap a strip of bandage tape around each of her fingertips. The tape she could wear around the clock, even when getting her hands wet. He made her go to school and church like this, too—an even greater mortification than the gloves. Sara was so nervous, shamed, and self-conscious, she bit her nails even more—right through the tape.

Relentless, his next recourse was physical pain. He put hot pepper sauce on each of Sara's fingers and let it dry. It not only burned her tender, infected fingers, but every time Sara put a finger to her mouth, it would burn her lips and her tongue as well. Still, Sara could not stop biting her nails, and she developed sores in her mouth and on her tongue from the burning of the pepper sauce.

Sara grew more and more anxious while her daddy grew more angry, frustrated, and determined—a dangerous mix for a mentally ill or possessed person. He told Sara, "I'll give you two weeks to stop biting your nails. If I see at the end of two weeks that you're still biting your nails, I'll give you ten lashes for every nail you've bitten!"

Now, I'm not a whiz at math, but I can calculate ten lashes times ten fingernails. That's one hundred lashes. This would nearly kill an adult, much less a small child, and Sara was a tiny, little, petite thing—the smallest child in her class throughout school.

Sara tried to stop, oh, how she tried.

She was terrified and traumatized all the more thinking all day, every day, for two weeks about the horrifically painful death sentence she was facing. The more he punished her for biting her nails, the more nervous and fearful she became, causing her to bite her nails all the more. She knew her daddy would, in fact, follow through with this sadistic punishment. He always did what he said he was going to do to his children—*always*.

Sara prayed her little prayer with more depth and fervency out of her anguish and terror over what was inevitable. "Now I lay me down to sleep. *I pray the Lord my soul to keep*," she whispered as she wept. "If I should die before I wake," thinking of her fate, "I pray the Lord my soul to take."

The two weeks passed and it was time for him to inspect Sara's nails. She shook with fear and was physically ill knowing what her fate would be at the hands of this evil man. She could not fathom in her mind how her own daddy, or anyone for that matter, could be so unfeeling, so merciless, so cruel, so *evil*. If she had never fully known injustice before at his hand, she would know it now, and it would sear a place so deep inside her that it would change her.

Sara had bitten all ten of her nails.

Her little body shivered with terror as she cried, her teeth chattering as if standing in sub-zero temperatures, naked.

Tears and pleading poured from her wide, blue eyes in terror as she watched him unbuckle his belt and dramatically pull it from his belt loops, demanding she pull down her panties and bend over his bed.

The look in his eyes was unnatural, as though an alien, something evil, had taken possession of his body.

She knew she would surely die that night in a horrifically painful, methodical, and sadistic manner. Then, where would she be? Would she end up in the everlasting, burning hell fervently preached in church, forever tortured by fire— never ending? Or would she go to heaven and be freed from him and his torture for good?

Little Sara just couldn't wrap her mind around the execrable evil threatening her as she cried and pleaded with him for mercy. The bile of sheer panic and terror was in her throat, choking her. At only a mere eight years old, life and death were held in precarious balance.

The punishment of one hundred lashes, as promised, began.

Sometime into the flogging, unable to bear the physical pain, Sara's mind "dissociated" from her body.[3]

> God knew before he created man, that men would perpetrate such evil against each other—even against their own—that they would all too quickly kill and destroy without some kind of protection in place for the mind and spirit. As a survival tool, God created in every one of us the amazing ability to psychologically disconnect our mind from our body when our body is under too severe a physical attack or trauma. It's what enables prisoners

of war, holocaust victims, and victims of other heinous crimes and serious traumas—like the violations of physical and sexual abuse—to be able to survive and still function under that degree of physical pain and trauma.

God's word tells us in Psalm 139:14 that we are "fearfully and wonderfully made," meaning intricately complex and amazing. Even today, as physicians and scientists continue to study the complexities of the human body, mind, and spirit, they are learning that there is still much to learn of the vast complexities of man.

Looking back, that fateful night was Sara's earlist recollection of dissociating, though she didn't know what it was at the time. She remembers only the beginning of that series of methodical beatings before her mind automatically moved into a dissociative state, seperating her from the trauma.

Her first conscious recollection in the aftermath was in the kitchen. She was lying face down across her mama's lap and crying as her mama applied a salve to Sara's shredded and bleeding legs and bottom. Sara's mama quietly cried with her as she worked and gently reassured her.

The memory of that most severe and horrifying flogging was forever branded into Sara mentally, psychologically, and physiologically. Today, when she recalls the beatings, her body automatically reacts with the same "body memory" each time—a prickly sensation that spreads across her bottom and down the back of her legs, progressing to a feverish sensation that reaches the soles of her feet. This, in turn, causes the bottoms of her feet to respond with a burning sensation, like the thermostat of her nerve endings had been turned up.

It was after that severe beating that Sara would often awake in the night with the burning sensation in the soles of her feet from toe to heel. It would feel as though the bottoms of her feet had been rubbed very rapidly for a long period, a miserable feeling. She would stick her feet out from under the covers to allow the night air to bathe and cool her feet. This was often not enough to eliminate the sensation. She would sometimes get up, go quietly into the bathroom, trying not to awaken her dad, close the door, and as quietly as possible fill the tub with enough cold water to submerge her feet. She would sit on the side of the tub, her feet covered by the cold water until it numbed her feet, eliminating the burning sensation. This continued for years. Even today, she sometimes sleeps with her feet outside the covers due to the recurring body memory.

There were times when Sara would be so overwhelmed with ever-present and varied physical sensations and pains, coupled with emotional anguish, intensive frustration and anger, that she would flail her arms as hard as she could across her bed in despair, beating the mattress with all her strength until there was nothing but defeat remaining in her. She'd fall on her bed weeping and exhausted, resignation her blanket.

Sara's world was constant trauma, "fight or flight," a continual heightened state of emotions. Her life was a perpetual roller-coaster ride, walking on eggshells at every waking moment, and demonic nightmares at night. An ever present fear engulfed and ruled her to the point that normal day-to-day activities, like school, were clouded. Her mind was often too crowded by fear and the effort to survive to take in the ordinary around her, whether at home, school, or church. Her mind was consumed with the extraordinary—surviving.

> When children live with enormous, on-going trauma, they will adopt some form of outward self-abuse that mimicks physically the emotional pain they are in. A cry for help; a way to 'feel'…It might be crouching in a corner and rocking, or banging their head against a wall. It might be pulling their hair out strand by strand, or their eyebrows and eye lashes. It might be nail biting or cutting themselves, or any other form of self-injury.

Sara began pulling out her eyebrows and eyelashes—more self-injury.[4]

One Sunday evening in church, the shame of this embarrassing self-abuse caught up with her. It was rare that she was allowed to sit with a friend during church, but this particular Sunday evening she was granted the privilege. Her friend's mama sat next to Sara, on her left.

After the drawn-out singing of the typical five verses from five hymns, Sara settled into her own little world. Her way of avoiding the booming declarations of hell resounding from the pulpit was to busy herself with silent activity and evasive thoughts. It became natural for her to busy herself with the habit of pulling out her eyebrows, then her eyelashes. She had opened a hymnal on her lap and watched as her tiny, pale brown hairs collected against the starkness of the white pages.

After a few moments, encased in her own thoughts, she was suddenly jerked back to reality when her friend's mama touched her arm. At her touch, Sara jumped and quickly raised her eyes to the woman, with shame and humiliation. A look of shock and disapproval was registered on the woman's face as she shook her head "no" at Sara, indicating she cease that abhorrent, destructive activity, and silently admonishing her.

Another humiliating habit in a growing list of self-injuries that Sara tried to hide from the world was a powerful, driven urge to make small, jerky movements with her right forearm and head—especially when she was overly anxious, tired, or overwhelmed, which was much of the time. With what seemed to be an invisible force controlling her body, she was driven to jerk her forearm in a chopping motion against whatever happened to be in front of her—the edge of a table, counter, or desk. She would jerk her head in short, hard nodding motions, her lower jaw tightened, which would leave her with aching jaws, neck, and headaches. She could hardly control these urges. It was as though a volcano of molten rage and hatred was shaking her very foundation, manifested physically in a feeble but fervent attempt to prevent a spewing eruption of hot, suppressed emotions.

As she grew older, she began to harbor fear that she had developed Tourette's Syndrome, a frightening disorder that she'd heard about on TV. She had looked it up in the encyclopedia to learn more about this horrifying, uncontrollable condition and was relieved that she appeared to have only a mild and intermittent case. Or perhaps she had something altogether different but equally as scary. She didn't know what she had and was too young to equate it with stress and anxiety caused by her daddy. She was doubly thankful that the atrocious cursing, silently directed at her daddy, was not the continual outbursts of obscenities the encyclopedia characterized with Tourette's. Still, she was fearful she must have some mild form of this condition and fearful it would grow to the unmanageable, gross proportions she read about. She knew for certain that should her silent cursing become outbursts, her daddy would most surely beat her to death. In her house, cursing, like drinking and smoking, was a damnable sin, right up there with murder and fornication—whatever that was. She had heard that word a lot in church but didn't really know what it meant. She just knew fornication had to be something unforgivable from the way the preacher screamed damnation about it.

If she wasn't jerking her arm or her head, or biting her nails, she was tearing up the inside of her cheeks and lips with her teeth, ripping and gnawing the skin off until she could taste the blood and her teeth ached. Her mouth was left raw, blistered, and scarred on the inside. The constant parade of self-injuries was not only perpetually painful and embarrassing, but also terribly exhausting and frustrating from the great emotional energy that self-injury consumes. But, hard as she tried, she just couldn't stop hurting herself. *What's wrong with me?* She would often wonder to herself, sensing that it was not normal behavior for a person to habitually inflict physical pain on their own body. She felt something *must* be wrong with *her*. She was just a child, too young to recognize or understand that the issues creating havoc in her mind, emotions, and body was not attributed to something being wrong with her, or something she had done wrong. The underlining, catastrophic problem was her *daddy*.

Nail biting and the list of other self-abuses followed Sara well into adulthood. Her nail biting was a constant embarrassment and constant effort to gain control over. Her driven need to incessantly jerk her head and forearm also created relentless difficulty for her. It was a daily challenge to accomplish the most simplistic tasks with her right hand—writing a check at the grocery store, making lists, writing a short note to a friend.

The urge to jerk her right arm was so powerful much of the time that she could hardly keep her pen on the paper—a daily, oftentimes hourly, challenge that sucked energy from her. She would have to consciously think about forcing herself to hold her arm still whenever she took up a pen. At times, when she was alone, tired and frustrated, she'd just give in to the urges until they seemed to have run their course, leaving her completely exhausted, but relieved.

It wasn't until 2001, when she discovered the blessed relief of prescription medication through her physician that she felt "normal" for the *first* time in her life, having battled *forty-one years* against the atrocities directly caused by the destruction of consistent childhood abuse. She wished that *someone* had told her about such medications early on. There was help! She is ever thankful for caring physicians and pharmaceutical scientists, who have dedicated themselves to helping others, like Sara, change their lives for the better. The right prescription medication has truly changed Sara's life in extraordinary ways toward healing and quality of life. She has witnessed firsthand how God uses *people*—including physicians, scientists, and therapists—to "work for the good" what evil meant to destroy. God promises in Romans 8:28, "…in all things God works for the good of those who love him, who have been called according to his purpose." In "all" things, He says—not in *some* things; in *all* things.

Chapter Six

Horrific nightmares tormented Sara's mind and emotions throughout the years, well into middle age. In addition to the repeated dream of her daddy holding her toddler brother upside down over the toilet, she had two other recurring and disturbing dreams as a child.

> *She was lying face up on a narrow cot in their living room, near the hallway opening. She was covered only by a thin, white, cotton night gown that reached her ankles. The dark rafters looming high above her, angled in crisscross, were enormous. The shiny, solid wood beams appeared powerful and imposing.*
>
> *Suddenly, she felt that one of the massive beams was within her arms. She felt the width and power, so all-encompassing within her tiny arms that she could*

not encircle it. She couldn't bring her arms together for
its enormity. Then the pulsating would begin. A slow,
rhythmic stretching and shrinking—modulated pulses
she could feel within her outstretched arms.

Although this repetitive dream occurred often as a young child, she can still feel the sensation in her arms today whenever she recalls the dream—indicative of a body memory indicating that something *real* had actually been within her little arms, too wide for her to encircle, and had pulsated on top of her, rendering her trapped. She cannot help but consider today that the powerful rafter in her arms had been in reality the actual power and enormity of a man—his body pulsating in her arms—leading her to also consider that she had very likely been sexually molested before she was old enough to conceptualize that kind of mature reality.

❤ ❤ ❤

By the time she was a preteen, the "rafter" nightmare had subsided and was replaced by another recurring dream that continued frequently for several years. She experienced the dream so often that she can still see every detail clearly in her mind today, as if she had just witnessed it with full visual acuity at a movie theater.

The era appeared to be seventeenth century. Sara watched as a young woman—whom she felt was herself—stared out across the water.

The young woman's cascading raven-blue hair
billowed in the warm salt air as she stood regally

along the breast-high wall of the ship's rustic, wooden deck. Her back to the crew, she looked out over the vast expanse of ocean. She was the only female aboard the massive cargo ship, but she felt no fear. It was a beautiful, sunny day that sparkled in the ocean tips like a valley of diamonds. Her brilliant blue, expertly tailored dress matched her eyes and mirrored the sea. She was at peace and reveled in the feel of the damp, cool breeze bathing her sun-warmed face.

Without warning, the bright sky was abruptly invaded by a heavy mass of dark, angry clouds. The air grew suddenly chilled. She turned around, peering across the expansive breadth of worn deck, and saw the island cliffs ahead, towering on the horizon.

She suddenly stood alone on the beach, unaware of and unconcerned with the ship's quiet departure. She peered up the sandy hill at the gargantuan, gray castle standing strong with the furious sky. She was here for a purpose, a mission that she steeled herself toward in strong determination.

Now inside the castle, she faced the length of the long, dark corridor so familiar. The hallway housed opposing doors on either side, each closed, cold, and eerily quiet, just as she had remembered them. She had traveled that length of passage countless times through her life, always with gripping fear that propelled her on to her destination at the other end—her place of light and safety. Each time she had passed along the narrow corridor, she kept her eyes straight ahead, focused on the pale light in the distance escaping from beneath the door and illuminating from the exit sign above it. She moved as quickly as she could without running. In her defiance against fear, she refused to run. She was determined to rule the fear instead of it ruling her.

What lay behind the closed doors on either side was terrifying. Dark spirits whispered out to her, beckoning her to open a door—any door—and enter. Fear crawled through her like a chill, threatening to choke her. The cold and darkness compelled her to run as fast as she could to the other end, to the light, but she walked, head high, determined that she would stand stronger than the fear. She turned neither to the right nor to the left as she moved forward.

For years, the warmth and security promised on the other side of that distant door had given her the courage to keep moving forward, despite her fears. But this time it was different. Evil had invaded her safe place and dared her to confront. This time she was on a mission of reckoning with evil that was long overdue. This time she was ready, determined.

At last, she reached her destination. With both hands flattened against the weighted door, she pushed through, blinded by the contrasting light that met her shadowed face.

The outer room was bright, clean, and neat, as it always had been. The patterned, tile floor of peach and apricot, intermixed with white, had always intrigued and captivated her attention. Through the years, she had spent countless hours studying the pattern and colors, always drawn to it, but not today. She hardly gave the pattern a glance or a thought. She stilled her eyes on the inner door—the place of reckoning she was compelled to push through and meet her mission head-on.

The inner room, small and rectangular, appeared the same as it always had. It displayed the same warm, patterned tile floor and gleaming white walls segueing from the outer room. Four, pale apricot stalls, their doors hung slightly open, ran the length of the narrow room along her right. Instead of peace and comfort that the inner room had always offered, this time fear gripped her heart and adrenaline surged through her chest and down her arms as she pushed her way determinedly into the first stall—and saw her.

There sat an old and hunched woman—a witch. Her heavily wrinkled face was leathery and dark with age of a million lifetimes. An ironing board stood before her, separating them. The old woman sat behind the board, working intently with the needle grasped in her gnarled, rugged fingers. She looked up, expectantly, into the face of the young woman as she entered, a subtle, evil smirk playing at her thin lips.

With quick foresight, just before the witch moved to attack, the young woman snatched the scissors from the ironing board and stabbed the two gleaming points into the witch's fleshy forearm. Then she snatched the piece of protruding skin at the puncture and ripped it down the length of the witch's arm, rendering her debilitated. Skinning her alive, strip by strip, she destroyed the evil.

It wasn't until the fall of 2006, when Sara sat down in obedience to God to pen her life story, that He opened the eyes of her understanding to the incredibly stunning realization that this recurring childhood dream was in actuality a *profound prophecy foretelling her own life journey* toward emotional healing, spiritual maturity, and ultimate freedom. A prognostication revealing the divine Trinity—Father, Son, and Spirit—ruling in her, that would span the years, from the time she was a young woman seeking healing, to the day she would become whole.

- *The seventeenth century era represents that the generational curses of sin, abuse, and evil had begun a long time ago—centuries.*
- *The ship represents the strong, well-built, sturdy vehicle (the Holy Spirit), that carried Sara safely across the turbulent seas of life to the place in time where she would ultimately meet all the years of evil and fear head-on and be equipped, ready and determined to boldly destroy it once and for all from her life, and from her generations to come.*
- *Her standing alone on the ship's deck symbolizes how only she alone could take a bold stand to declare the abuses, sins, and evils that had been perpetrated against her, impacting and shaping her life. No one else could do this for her. Others could only support, encourage, and aid her along the way. This support is represented by the crew on the ship that she had been aware of and had greatly depended on to help carry her across the sea of life.*
- *The breeze across her face, as she stood along the railing of the ship's deck, is the breath of God, bathing and refreshing her along her far and arduous journey. The same wind propels the ship across the distance, over the turbulent sea of life,*

expertly steering her toward her divine destination and purpose.

- *Standing regal, her face was turned upward to the bright and warming sun (Jesus).*
- *Her splendid, royal blue dress (matching the blue of her eyes and the blue of the sea), master tailored to shroud her expertly from shoulders to feet is representative of her wounds, and also how God has clothed her as a princess, the daughter of the King of Kings, from the moment she accepted His Son, Jesus, into her heart, and wrapped her expertly in the Holy Spirit.*

   This is how she would eventually come to see herself—and dress herself spiritually—as God sees her: His beloved, His princess, clothed in righteousness, standing with confidence, knowing who she is in Christ.

   The color blue is also used frequently throughout the Bible to describe the color of a wound (Proverbs 20:30). It also describes the sky, heaven, and the Holy Spirit.

- *The beautiful, sunny day that sparkled like a valley of diamonds on the ocean represents the great, priceless, limitless treasury of beautiful and brilliant people Sara would amass along her life journey. Strong, loving, caring people ever before her, in her line of vision—both those who would assist her, as well as those she would assist, those who would bring her further along the journey, and those she would bring further along.*

- *The dark, angry clouds and cold breeze invading the warmth and bright beauty of the day is indicative of the spiritual warfare that rages—even today—throughout the world, directly affecting us (distracting, clouding, and cooling our walk with God), no matter where we are standing or what we are doing.*

• *The enormous, gray castle looming over the beach and standing in harmony with the dark, raging sky represents both Sara's childhood home and church as one. Her family had spent endless hours alone at church through many years, while her daddy did volunteer work there. The enormous church, whose dark corridors she had roamed countless times alone, had become her second home. The family often ate there and the children played and slept there while he worked, late into the nights. Having no regard for his children's need of sleep, it was not uncommon for Sara and her siblings to find a pew to curl up on and fall sleep (often cold), disrupted when their daddy decided it was time to go home.*

To Sara, both home and church often felt encapsulated in darkness and evil, cold and engulfing. Both places she would often revisit (emotionally), via the ship of the Holy Spirit, to face the evil head-on in her mission to destroy it. Dark places where she would return with determination, undaunted purpose, growing strength, and character, to seek out and destroy the innermost evil that had dominated her for so long.

• *The long, dark and cold corridor represents the pathway, the journey of her life within the confines of her outer and inner prisons, leading to the bright, warm, and safe place at the end (healing, restoration, and freedom). The eyes of her heart were ever focused on the faint light beyond her reach, illuminating from beneath the doorway and "exit" sign to freedom. A place where her innermost room would be cleaned out, and all the evil and ugliness festering inside would finally be annihilated.*

- *The faint light illuminating from beneath the destination door and the exit sign above aptly symbolizes the ever-burning, faint light of hope and exit-way from hell, always in her line of vision, straight ahead, encouraging and prompting her to keep walking forward until she reached that light of truth and freedom.*

- *The multiple, closed doors running the length of the corridor—her journey—to the left and the right, symbolizes the demons that were ever present around her, wooing her, yet unable to touch her unless she willingly turned to the left or to the right, opened a door and entered into their dwelling places. Proverbs 4:25 and 27 says, "Let your eyes look straight ahead, fix your gaze directly before you. Do not swerve to the right or the left; keep your foot from evil."*

- *The outer room at the end of the corridor, her destination, signifies the safe and well lit place within her heart where the Holy Spirit reigns.*

- *The gleaming, white walls throughout is synonymous with the purity of her heart, her motives, her desires, her dreams, her purposes.*

- *The warm-colored, patterned floor that so enraptured her and kept her attention, represents the immense creativity God had so beautifully and* precisely placed within her at birth, and which permeates her entire being—mind, emotion, spirit—influencing how she thinks, feels, and responds. This being the 'flooring,' it symbolizes how foundational the creativity is to her.

- The innermost door represents the entrance to the deepest places within her—her core—that housed several stalls (compartments). Each was well lit, clean, tidy, and comfortable, except for the first stall. This one contained and restrained all the fears, ugliness, and evil she had had to continually stuff inside through the years and keep buried for so long.

- The old woman—the witch—represents the evil one himself (Satan), and all the evil and fear she had had to keep from others for so many years, intermixed with all the hatred and anger she had harbored against her daddy.

- The sewing that the witch was intent upon is symbolic of Satan's steady and eternal binding work to destroy Sara since birth that she had to continually battle against.

- The ironing board separating them represents the divider between good and evil that Sara had chosen not to cross—time and again.

- The sharp, two-pointed scissors that were easily accessible on the ironing board, represents the sharp sword of the Lord—His Word. "For the word of God is living and active. Sharper than any double-edged sword" (Hebrews 4:12).

- The penetration of the scissors into the witch's flesh is the strike of truth against the lies and evil.

> *"...penetrates even to dividing soul and spirit, joints and marrow" (Hebrews 4:12).*
> - *The stripping away of flesh represents the exposing and annihilation of the evil one. When stripped away, there is no evil and ugliness remaining, giving way to true freedom of heart and mind.*

Wow! What a profoundly amazing and detailed revelation to Sara! God had been showing her all along, throughout her childhood, by way of this dream—her destiny—how she would choose to persevere, work hard, and keep moving forward in the face of her ever-surrounding fears. And that she would eventually be a conqueror, made *free* from her bondages. However, that victorious day of true freedom would not come for many years—well into her adulthood.

Chapter Seven

By the time Sara had entered puberty and began to show signs of becoming a young woman, she was well conditioned to the absolute of obeying her daddy. So, when he began coming into the children's room at night, uncharacteristically kind and attentive to Sara, under the guise of wanting to rub her back, she was far too fearful to say a word, much less to tell him she didn't like it and wanted him to stop. She felt terribly invaded and sickened every time his hands pushed beneath her pajama top, on her bare back, as she lay face down on her bed.

She hated his touch. It burned a new kind of rage within her. She wanted him to die.

As horrific as the physical abuse had been for years, this

new horror he hinted at with his hands, and uncharacteristic soothing words, felt deathly sickening inside Sara.

> There are not human words adequate to describe the nauseous depths of feelings of hatred, helplessness, imprisonment, and injustice that a girl or a woman experiences when being touched by a man against her will – not to mention her own biological daddy, who was supposed to love and protect her! Sexual abuse invades and robs to the very core of your being. It is the worst possible abuse, with far deeper and longer damaging effects. It is beyond words.

Sara had no one to protect her and no one to whom she could go for help. Her mama loved her openly and deeply, but she didn't protect Sara. She was too immobilized with fear and intimidation herself. Sara believes her mama had been brainwashed by the legalistic beliefs and practices of their church, hand in hand with what appeared to be the societal attitude of that generation. Abuse was not openly discussed nor openly defined. There were no hotlines to call. There were no broadcast messages that said, "Tell someone."

Nevertheless, as a mature adult revisiting her childhood, Sara grew to believe it had been grossly wrong, irresponsible, and negligent of her mama to allow the abuses by her husband against their five children—no matter his influence, or the church's and society's influences, at the time. In her view, her mama had been an adult, making conscious, adult choices, too—against the safety and well-being of her children—by not intervening to protect them against her husband.

Sara grew to believe that the childhood abuses she and her siblings had survived were also the direct fault and responsibility of the church they were raised in. It had been far more a 'cult' religion than a Godly religion by way of their legalistic beliefs and practices that had knowingly or ignorantly encouraged and supported abuse of authority. She recognized that their childhood church was one who had given true, Godly Christianity such a bad name, negating the true freedom, hope, love, and relationship that the Word of God and His characteristics embody.

As a child, there was no one Sara could talk to except for God, and she talked to Him a lot. She prayed without ceasing—for deliverance, hope, and a future free from her daddy. She poured through the scriptures that fed her hope. She spent a lot of time in the Psalms, feeling less alone by hearing the despair of the Psalmists.

In Jeremiah 29, she read the letter that the prophet Jeremiah sent to those in exile. This gave her further hope that the promises she read might be hers, as well:

> *"For I know the plans I have for you," declares the Lord, "plans to prosper you and not to harm you, plans to give you hope and a future. Then you will call upon me and come and pray to me, and I will listen to you. You will seek me and find me when you seek me with all your heart. I will be found by you," declares*

the Lord, "and will bring you back from captivity"
Jeremiah 29:11.

Sara *had* to believe the scriptures she read again and again were true because God was her only hope and her only sounding board.

By the age of thirteen, she had heard the plan of salvation a gazillion times. At least three or more times a week the messages of doom reverberated from the pulpit warning of an everlasting, burning hell and the need to repent and be born again—to be saved. Yes, Sara would learn for herself, as an adult, that these *are* Biblical truths, but she had been given nothing more than fear. She had not been taught the *whole* of the truths: the all-encompassing love, mercy, and grace of an ever-present, long-suffering, and compassionate God. She had not heard about an intimate, loving relationship with Christ. She had not been taught about all the amazing characteristics of a loving, righteous God who is Father to all who accept His Son, Jesus, into their heart by faith. There were only messages of fear—and rules—from the pulpit and from her daddy that the children were inundated with daily.

Sara already lived in her own hell, created by her daddy. She couldn't imagine living all of eternity in a hell of fire and torture, as well—never to have hope or freedom. But there it was, the truths of sin, hell, and separation from God written in the same book where she also read of hope, the promises of God, eternal joy, unconditional love, and abundant life that comes with accepting Jesus Christ as Savior.

So, it must *all* be true—the *whole* Word—not just in part.

She knew she couldn't accept only selected portions of God's Word, as her daddy had appeared to do by his teachings—demanding only laws and rules against the threat and reality of harsh punishments. She had to accept *all* of God's Word or none of it because it was either all truths or all lies. How could one divide up the Bible as partial truths, accepting some of it and throwing out the rest? Who has that right, that authority over God? No, she had to believe the entire Bible was true, because she desperately needed real hope and a certain future of joy and freedom that the Word spoke of. She must believe that God would keep His promises if she were to sincerely ask Him to forgive her sins and be her Savior. She wanted His promises, not just to avoid a horrid, eternal hell. She wanted to gain true joy and freedom. What did she have to lose by believing all of God's Word to be truth and walking in the hope and faith of His promises? What other hope did this life offer her? None. Absolutely none. God was truly her only hope, her only future, and most certainly her only sounding board.

On a Wednesday night, at the age of thirteen, sitting in the back seat of her family's car as they traveled home from church, her face pressed against the cool glass and her eyes staring up at the stars as she often did, Sara silently and sincerely prayed. She asked God to forgive her sins, to be her Savior, and to secure a place for her in heaven. She asked Him to bring her freedom and joy—escape from her daddy.

Trusting in God was Sara's *only* hope in life and in death. There was no one else who had the power to deliver her or to give her a hope and a future. Sara took that hope and that quiet, simple salvation experience to heart that night.

It not only gave her hope in death, but hope in life, as well. Accepting Jesus by sheer faith into her heart would not guarantee protection of her physical body, but it *would* guarantee protection of her mind and spirit against all manner of evil that would soon come against her.

♥ ♥ ♥

There was an imposing, spiritual contradiction raging within the walls of Sara's house. Her daddy not only took his family to their church every time the doors were open, but he also practiced dark activities that opened wide the doors for Satan to enter and dwell among the family. His pursuits inadvertently brought Sara face to face with the spirit world and gave her uncommon insight at a young age into the spiritual war that rages at this very hour. The same war that's been raging since the great angel of light, Lucifer, was cast out of heaven along with his angels, now called demons (Read Revelation 12:7–9, Romans 14:11, and Ephesians 6:12).

She was fifteen-years-old when her daddy began to practice the craft of hypnosis and used her as his subject. Even with her lack of knowledge about this practice, she had an acute sense within her that this practice—*in the format he was using it*—was from an evil and dangerous source. Only God could have given one so unaware and innocent such insight. She was terrified of what horrors he would render against her if he also took authority over her mind. She outwardly cooperated out of fear, but did not allow her mind to be taken in, and God protected her mind.

He delved deeper into spiritual darkness when he began to practice what is known as astro travel or astral projection.

With this out-of-body practice, the demons had a fully open invitation to set up camp among Sara's family, and particularly Sara, as she was the object of her daddy's obsession.[5]

He shared with Sara that, during his astral state, he could "fly" all around, out in the world, and could see everything below him. He said it felt like a powerful force when his spirit returned to his body. Appalled and frightened by this imagery, and the supernatural implications, she would imagine him flying in his altered spirit-state into her room and hovering over her like an evil spirit, watching her while she slept. Terribly frightened, she did not even want to consider what he might be thinking and contemplating as he hovered over her. She considered that if he had the supernatural power to leave his body and fly around, then he must also have supernatural power to hurt her further. It was unthinkable to her that he would have this added dimension of power and control that he could use against her.

The days of Sara's life were growing darker and heavier with the oppression of evil as Satan was allowed to gain more and more control over her daddy's thoughts, reasoning, and actions—conscious choices he was making.

At night in her bed, she began having the most terrifying experiences. Just after she would lie down, a great heaviness would come over her entire body, so heavy that her body would be immobile, as though paralyzed. She was unable to move at all. She could only see and hear. She could see into the lighted living room beyond her doorway and hear the muted sounds from the TV, but could not feel her body at all. She was unable to move. It was so terrifying, she would try to scream out to her mama who sat in the living room, just a few feet away, but blocked from view by the dividing wall. But she had no voice. She would try with all her might to fight against the heaviness, but she was paralyzed from head to toe. She would fight against it with everything she had until it would suddenly leave her, just as quickly as it had come over her. This happened night after night. Sara became terrified to lie down. She fought sleep and only slept from sheer exhaustion. She wondered, as an adult, if perhaps her daddy's traveling, evil spirit had played a part in this.

One night, something much greater happened when the heavy weight pinned her down and paralyzed her. As she fought against it, she suddenly began to hear a great chorus of hideous screaming—the kind of bone chilling screams of people suffering merciless torture. A sound so animal heinous that it was even beyond the screams of pain she and her siblings endured whenever her daddy was whipping Matt.

She fought all the harder against the heaviness, the horrific screaming, and the paralysis controlling her body. Then a vision appeared: a great fire and a massive cavern of bottomless darkness from where the fire and howling were coming. Sara had come face to face with the reality of hell.

Then Satan revealed to her spirit a great power she could possess if she were to simply accept it from him—the supernatural foresight of a clairvoyant, a medium, seeing and forecasting the future. Sara knew in that moment that her eyes and ears had been awakened to the spirit realm of darkness whose control base is Hades, and whose practices are deceit and devastation. She felt the spiritual powers he offered, that she could possess and use in life. She had never had power of any kind, at all. Her daddy held all the power. Having power of her own was appealing, but the present control over her body, strapped to her bed by an invisible force, was far too terrifying to give in to his wooing and offering. She knew inside she would be making a terrible, life-changing choice if she accepted his offer of this power.

She fought all the harder to escape his heaviness and the world of peril she was witnessing, when suddenly a great, pure Light appeared from above and to the right. It revealed an all-encompassing peace, rest, and purity she knew in her heart to be the presence and greater power of God. His Light drew her spirit eyes and ears toward Him and away from the evil, and offered her peace, hope, beauty, love, and freedom. All of these pure qualities were interwoven in His very presence, as if He himself were actually the very essence of all these things in their purest form. Encased in His presence, Sara chose God and all that He was emanating to her with an unspoken but certain promise, and the heaviness immediately lifted from her body.

Later in life, Sara would look back on this rare experience—the uncommon insight into the spirit world and the choice she was given by Satan—and see the likeness to Jesus' experience found in Matthew 4:1–9.

> *Then Jesus was led by the Spirit into the desert to be tempted by the devil... The devil took him to a very high mountain and showed him all the kingdoms of the world and their splendor. "All this I will give you,"* *he said, "If you will bow down and worship me."*

Sara was given a life-altering choice that night when Satan

revealed himself and his limited power to her, and God had countered with His own almighty, Holy presence. Like Jesus, she had been given a choice to accept Satan's offer or to choose the right—the light, peace, safety, and promise of the Most High God who is love incarnate, the author, founder, creator of all things.

Just as Sara had given her heart, her hope, and her life to God through Jesus at the age of thirteen, sitting in the backseat of her parent's car, she again made the choice to keep her allegiance to Him.

But Satan is persistent.

The evil one, Lucifer, had been granted reign in Sara's house, through the doors her daddy had voluntarily opened into the spirit world by way of his ungodly behaviors and practices. As long as Satan roams the earth before Jesus returns, he will continue to be persistent in trying to draw us and entice us to his side in an effort to deceive, devour, and destroy all that is good, righteous, and whole. God's Word is very clear about the very real presence of the evil one and how he operates.

Sara's daddy, under the influence of Satan, was also determined to have her and completely possess her as his own. This was only the beginning of a great spiritual war Sara would be trapped in and battling against for many years to come.

Chapter Eight

Sara continued to pray and weep, pour over the scriptures and hope for a future free from her daddy. While many other young people were occupied with school, grades, sports, boyfriends, dating, the hope of college, career, marriage, and family, Sara's only hope and longing in life was to live to see adulthood, to be free from her daddy and the evil and fear that was her life.

She daydreamed of the time when she would be a grownup, living free on her own, under no other person's power and control. She would envision herself in her own apartment, which would conjure up feelings of joy and pleasure at even the most mundane of chores ... grocery shopping, cleaning her home ... with a freedom unlike she had ever known, except in her daydreams. For the first time in

her life she would feel a sense of ownership by being out
on her own. It was a powerful feeling as she presently felt
no ownership of anything. She could not even own her own
emotions—even those her daddy tried to control.

She longed for that day of real freedom. All she dreamed
for her future was freedom. If she just had freedom, living apart
and independent from anyone's demands or power over her, she
would truly have all that she would ever need, she surmised in
her innocence. Her childlike dreams and childlike faith kept her
moving through the dark days, months, and years.

The abuse and evil was so prominent in her daily life that
it's amazing Sara even made it through school at all, much
less graduated with decent grades, which testifies to the mind
God had placed in her at birth. She was so immersed in trying to survive to see adulthood and escape her daddy and evil
that everything else in her peripheral was a fog. Many of the
common events of childhood were simply erased from her
recollection—perhaps never to be recovered.

> When fighting for your life and surviving trauma,
> there is no room left in the conscious mind to take
> in the normal day-to-day experiences.

She lost many years from her memory of "normal" activities and events of her childhood. Most prevalent in her
mind were the blatant experiences of terror and trauma she
survived and many of the experiences associated with her
church—both good and bad. She has only sketchy memo-

ries of first grade, associated with fear and punishment, but cannot recall a teacher…just some looming silhouette in her mind's eye. Equally sketchy memories of second grade were also infused with fear. Third, fourth, and fifth grades, coinciding with the heaviest years of terror, are completely missing from her memory altogether. Memories of school, teachers, peers, and their associated "normal" activities are just…gone. The next year of school that she was able to recall was sixth grade, coinciding with when she was entering puberty and the physical abuses had stopped.

What *was* seared into her memory of those otherwise missing years was being terrified of what might happen to her at any given time at the hands of her daddy. She spent her days at school in fear of teachers and students and always dreading the hour her daddy would arrive home from work, promptly at 5:30 p.m. She never knew what the evenings would bring. She moved through her days jumpy and intimidated, highly self-conscious and introverted (except with her closest friends), and fearful of going to sleep because of the nightmares.

She moved through her days and nights carefully, as though she was walking over broken glass. She never knew from moment to moment what might cause her daddy to react toward her with irritation or anger resulting in certain punishment. She even worried about supper—that she might not like something on her plate and would be forced to eat it, gagging through the meal. He always insisted that the children clean their plates, no matter what. If not, he'd make them sit at the table until they finished every bite—no matter how late—or be whipped. Sometimes they sat at the table through the evening, trying to force the food down to avoid punishment.

Her mama was an excellent southern cook and Sara loved most everything her mama prepared for supper. But occasionally her daddy would require a meal that he particularly liked but was near impossible for Sara and her siblings to force down—liver and onions, and sauerkraut were the two worst. On these evenings, punishment was a certainty. Just knowing ahead of time what supper she was faced with could make her ill, knowing that she'd be sick one way or the other—either from trying to force the bitter taste down (and trying to keep it down), or from the punishment that would surely follow if she didn't clean her plate. It was a no win situation.

What's wrong with me that I just can't stay focused and stay out of trouble? Sara thought to herself. *Why am I such a bad kid, always getting in trouble?* Most of the time, she didn't understand why she was in such trouble that he'd be so cruel. *Why doesn't he love me? Am I so bad? Why can't I get my schoolwork done? Why can't I get better grades? What's wrong with me?*

Day after day, little by little, Sara's spirit was being crushed. She was being taught that she was unlovable and of little worth. She believed her mama loved her; but still, that wasn't enough. The displeasure she seemed to regularly elicit from her daddy far outweighed the affirmations from her mama.

♥ ♥ ♥

Although higher education beyond high school was discouraged by her daddy, he was adamant about good grades, whipping the children for grades lower than a C. Yet, he had no regard for college education. He didn't see the point of advanced education and thought it useless in securing a decent job. In his narrow opinion, a high school diploma was all that one needed. He didn't care what his children aspired to and the avenue necessary to achieve their dreams. He only cared about his own opinions. Certain that he was right in every matter he spoke of, he expected his children to adopt his views without dispute, or pay a high price.

Despite his discouragement, Sara longed to be an elementary school teacher. She constantly dreamed of a classroom setting and would playact as teacher. She loved children and she loved mothering. She would envision a classroom full of children behind her as she marked neatly across the chalkboard. She loved the tapping sound that the chalk made as her teachers rapped against their blackboards. At home, she'd take a metal hairpin and pretend it was her chalk. She'd tap it across her mama's lengthy vanity mirror as if she were writing on a chalkboard, teaching.

Her daddy wouldn't hear of such dreams. He believed that working a job or trade following high school was far more important than college. He even encouraged the children to begin earning money as early as the law would allow—fourteen—except for a paper route, Sara's first job, at age twelve. She shared a route with Allie, and her brothers shared a paper route, too.

Every Saturday and Sunday morning at 4:00 a.m., their daddy would abruptly wake them with David Bowie's *Fame* pulsating at an ear-splitting volume through the house. Quickly up, they'd roll-n-wrap their papers in the living room floor, then take off on their bicycles by 5:00 a.m. to deliver throughout their neighborhood.

They were allowed to keep the money they earned, but never taught how to manage it. There was no instruction in saving, budgeting, or how to balance a checkbook, so they spent it. It was in Sara's high school accounting course that she learned these necessary basics.

At fourteen, she worked through the summer for a favorite aunt who owned a beauty shop and who was always kind and very generous. As an adult reflecting back, Sara was certain that her aunt had felt pity and sadness for the children and wanted to do whatever she could to make their lives a little brighter. Especially at Christmas, she was extravagant in giving gifts to Sara and her siblings, and felt badly for the children that their daddy would never allow a Christmas tree in their house.

In all the years that Sara and her siblings lived at home, there was never a Christmas tree. She enjoyed her first Christmas tree as an adult in her own home. Her daddy subscribed to the belief that the Christmas tree originated in sacrilegious ceremony, and he proclaimed this news at every opportunity—instead of Christ's birth—and that he would not have a Christmas tree in *his* house.

Whether this legend of the tree's origin was true or not, it didn't matter to him that Christianity had adopted it for good—as a symbol of the light of Christ and His gift to the world. The children did, however, receive gifts on Christmas morning—one of the few truly exciting days in their home during a calendar year. But getting gifts was the limit to their celebrating Christmas. Despite the hard-core, legalistic religious practices in their home, day in and day out, there were no stories read, nor talk about, Christ's birth. Her daddy would not celebrate Christ's birth at Christmas because he believed that December was not the *actual* season in which Jesus was born. Again, it mattered not to him that Christianity at large embraced December as the holy season to celebrate Christ's birth. Strangely though, the children were always allowed to don Halloween costumes and go trick-or-treating every October 31!

♥ ♥ ♥

At sixteen, she joined the work-study program at school, which allowed her to work in the afternoons and only attend school in the mornings. The entry-level job she secured was at one of the two largest newspapers competitively serving the state from their capitol city. It was no small city and the first time Sara had ever truly been out in the world on her own.

She relished this newfound freedom she had gained simply because she was now driving on her own, and working out in the world. Like working, her daddy never discouraged driving, but actually encouraged it. She got her learner's permit when she was only fourteen, her restricted license as soon as she turned fifteen. So, by the time she turned sixteen, she had had two years of driving experience and was very comfortable going solo. Her daddy had no problem with her having the freedom to drive herself to school and work. It was a taste of freedom that she had so longed and prayed for, but only a tease. She still had to go home each night after work.

Until that point in time, she had lived such an isolated and restricted life that she didn't quite understand all the attention she was suddenly getting from the men where she worked—men she passed on the busy, downtown streets, men she passed along the aisles in the stores, men she worked with ... It was both scary and compellingly enticing. The attention made her feel good and valued. She had never gotten affirmations of love or the fatherly affection that a daddy is supposed to give to his daughter. She had a deep, insatiable hunger for attention that she simply did not have the insight or maturity to understand. There were foundational things missing inside her from having had no loving, caring male influence in her life.

When Sara fell in love for the first time, it was with a young man where she worked. David was ten years older than Sara, divorced, and daddy to a toddler girl. Sara was a naive sixteen-year-old and he was an experienced twenty-six-year-old. He was very attractive, funny, caring, and very attentive to Sara. He made her feel valued and cherished. He was respectful and he was sincere in his attraction to her. He encouraged her to spend time with him as allowed during the work day. They took breaks together, traveled to a nearby park or the cubbyhole café nearby for lunch. He wooed Sara's heart and she followed, like a puppy, famished for love and attention. It was easy to fall in love—too easy.

He was very kind and humorously flirtatious with Sara—always making her laugh—but he never tried to woo her into bed. He sincerely liked Sara and quickly grew to care for her genuinely, with respect for her innocence and the highly restrictive life she lived under her daddy's stringent authority.

David gave her little gifts now and then, which she had to take great care to hide from her daddy—a 45 record of a popular Elvis love song mirroring what David said he felt for Sara, a single bouquet of flowers, and eventually a pretty little promise ring hugging a small diamond. Her first diamond. Her first love. Her first real hope of a future. Her first real hope of escape—and freedom. She longed to wear the ring proudly and openly but she had to hide that, too. She knew her daddy would never approve, but worse, he would be a madman over it.

David and Sara entertained thoughts and discussions of running away together. He was always kind and attentive, never forcing himself on her and always concerned over the desperate and disparaging life she was entrapped in. David was a gentleman who displayed genuine care and respect. She had never had that modeled by her daddy. David represented to her everything she could ever want or need in a companion, she thought. As she quickly grew to love and trust him, she wanted to spend the rest of her life by his side. Experiencing a fulfillment she had never before known, she was too naive to recognize the fundamental things missing inside her that prompted her desperate hunger for attention and appreciation. She grew more and more addicted to the attention David gave her, more hungry for his love and more hungry for the value he showed for her. She became increasingly dissatisfied with the little time they had together. She was too young and had been too restricted from the world to consider or understand how life choices and experiences shape a person. All she cared about was the attention and care David showed her. Nothing else mattered to Sara, except escaping her daddy.

In the stolen time that she and David had through the workweek, he was always more focused on her than on himself. He did share that he had been married, and divorced just after his daughter was born. He displayed much enthusiasm over his responsibility in caring for his toddler. He shared equal custody with his ex-wife.

It was apparent how much he loved his daughter. She was his pride and joy. Sara got to see this firsthand when David brought her to the park one afternoon. They spread a blanket on the ground and had a picnic. With an element of jealousy mixed with heartache and joy, Sara watched the two of them play together—a confusing, bittersweet mix of emotions for her. She couldn't help but wish she had had a daddy who openly loved and cared for her like David cared for his daughter. It saddened her as she considered all that she had missed by not having a loving daddy, though she couldn't quite separate or understand all the thoughts and feelings that stirred inside her. She was still too young to grasp the deep level of grief she would come to embrace in her adult years at not having a daddy who loved her.

That afternoon at the park was like a fairytale to Sara. She could easily imagine slipping into the role of step-mommy to his precious daughter, and wife to him.

David shared very little of his own life or past with Sara when they had opportunity to sit and talk. He was more interested in talking about her than himself. She would ask him questions and he would always be open with his answers but volunteered little. Sara didn't care about his past; she just wanted a future with him. That was enough for her. Where he had come from or what life he had led prior to Sara carried little weight with her.

He had seen no reason to share with Sara the recent and rather serious relationship he had had with a woman his own age, who also worked at the newspaper. After all, it was over just before he met Sara.

Cassie never had reason to cross young Sara's path at work. She worked in a different area of the paper altogether. However, after a time well into Sara and David's growing friendship, Sara began to hear snippets of rumors about Cassie when co-workers began cajoling him about "robbing the cradle," and how Cassie was becoming more irate over his attention to a mere sixteen-year-old. But David didn't care about the rumors, the haranguing, or Cassie's jealousy. He didn't care what Cassie or anyone else thought about his interest in Sara. His attention remained focused on her and protective of her.

The "office buzz" began snaking through the building. It grew with whispered talk of David's fixation on the young and naive *child*. The talk was juicy, as most office gossip is. The subject enticed even greater interest when the highly tempered and jealous Cassie demanded that David stop seeing Sara. Evidently, the relationship between he and Cassie was still volatile and the tie not completely severed—at least from Cassie's viewpoint.

Unbeknown to Sara, Cassie went into a jealous rage toward David. In her anger, she decided to locate Sara's home phone number through personnel records. She boldly called Sara's parents and informed them that a twenty-six-year-old man at the newspaper was having a relationship with their sixteen-year-old daughter. Cassie could not have known the consequence of that one phone call, and the degree to which it would cost Sara.

When she arrived home from work that evening, she

was totally unprepared for how her world was about to come crashing down. In a rage, her daddy confronted her, interrogated her, and told her she would not be going back to work there and would never see "that man" again. Sara was terrified and devastated over the sudden turn of events. One minute she was in love and hopeful of a future when she would be free to love, and the next minute all her hopes and dreams were destroyed. Out of the strength of her love for David, she boldly pled her case in the face of her daddy's outrage. It was the first time in Sara's life that she had consciously chosen to stand up against her daddy. Love was a powerful force.

Her daddy was so maddened that he put Sara and her mama in the car and drove out searching for David. Her daddy was going to kill him. Thankfully—much to Sara's relief—he never found David. She couldn't even imagine the potential altercation between the two of them, or what could have turned out to be an even more devastating outcome.

Most disturbing and unnerving to Sara was the realization that her daddy was not in a rage protective of his daughter's safety and virginity, but rather in a *jealous* rage at the thought of another man putting his hands on the body he believed was meant solely for himself.

When they arrived back home, late that evening, Sara's daddy hammered her with probing questions for hours into the early morning. He insisted she tell him what sexual things they had done and drilled into her that she was not in love; she was in lust. Sara was terrified of her daddy but bravely continued to defend her love for David, fueled by the rare gift she had found in his love for her. She stood her ground boldly against her daddy, but he was the master of manipulation, debate, and determination. He would never give in or give up—He would never give *her* up.

He refused to believe Sara had not engaged in sex. In truth, she had not even come close to having sex. David had been very flirtatious and attentive to Sara, but all in all, he had displayed a respectful affection that grew to be genuine care and love for her. He never once took advantage of her physically, emotionally, or mentally, unlike Sara's own daddy. It was solely her daddy who had taken those wrong advantages.

Sara continued to boldly plead her love for David, but to no avail. Her daddy was determined to dispel what he considered her "fantasies of love" and keep her from David at all costs. No matter what he had to resort to, he was adamantly purposed to change her way of thinking, even if it meant Sara would never again be out of his or her mama's sight.

Hours had passed when her daddy began to get desperate, realizing he was getting nowhere with Sara. In his relentless determination for her to succumb to his will and his way of thinking, he whipped out his Bible and began to rip out the pages one by one, screaming at Sara that the Word meant nothing to her and that she was in lust—in sin—not in love.

Sara was stunned at what she was witnessing. With disbelief and horror at the outright physical disrespect of God's Word, she watched him rage on, ripping out page after page. In Sara's mind, this was the ultimate irreverence to God. She had been brutally beaten for simply running in God's house as a child, and here he was, taking the Holy written Word of God and destroying it for what appeared to Sara to be his own relentless cause: her allegiance to him. Her frantic mind raced. *How could he display such unabashed insolence toward*

God, after all the years he had hammered into us the absolute reverence and respect for His Word, His name, and His house? How in the world could he possibly justify this insane act and still defend what he had terrifyingly instilled in us?

This wouldn't be the last time she saw such blatant contradictions between his talk and his walk.

Sara knew the real truth about her conduct with David in the stolen hours she had spent with him, talking, eating, daydreaming. She was innocent, still a virgin, and she was, in fact, in love. Sex and lust had played no part in it. Nevertheless, her daddy continued to insist that he *knew* Sara had had sexual relations with David. He went so far as to command that Sara's mama take her to the doctor the very next day to be examined, to learn if she was still a virgin. Sara didn't quite understand how the doctor would know one way or the other, and the simple thought of an examination of her private parts was terrifying. However, if the doctor could truly tell if she had engaged in sex, she already knew what he would find. She was still a virgin.

No matter what she said to her daddy in this defense, he did not and would not believe her. He was out of his mind with jealousy and desperation over the thought of losing her to another man. He was fearful that she was truly in love and no longer willing to yield to his will. Had Sara understood the significance of the power she held at that moment, to fully defy her daddy and walk out, she believes he would have most certainly followed and killed her, or done serious injury to her, out of his jealous wrath and desperation, and his need to have complete control.

Sara was terrified and exhausted in those early dawn hours and knew she would never convince him of her true and innocent love for David. She knew she would never escape her daddy unless she ran away, died, or he died. She was consumed by the greatest grief she had ever known, grief at the thought of never seeing David again, and the deepest hatred she had ever held for her daddy.

Defeated and depleted, she gave in to him, rightly believing she would never win. He always won. He always had the power and the control, and she held so little—none that she was aware of. It sickened her even more when he immediately called his best friend and pompously declared how he had "rescued" his daughter from sin and destruction, elevating himself to hero status, proving to be the wise, upright, and Godly man that he believed himself to be. She loathed him all the more in his eagerness and pride at having won the battle, then boasted to others. Again, it was his total gain and her total loss. But the worst was yet to come.

In the days that followed, he continued to rage and interrogate her—unable or unwilling to believe that David had not had his way with her. She was terribly shaken with fear of her daddy, grief over losing David, and exhaustion at his persistence and her lack of sleep. In his boundless absorption of jealousy and out of his own fears, he had to further prove his rule, his reign, his power, his possession over Sara. He went through her room in a tizzy, gathered up everything meaningful to her that he could quickly put his hands on, took everything outside to the back yard and burned it all up! He might as well have thrown Sara in that pile and burned her up, too. She wanted nothing more than to die—or for him to die. She detested him all the more, inflamed by feelings of raw injustice he continually evoked in her. *She hated him.*

Chapter Nine

Sara grew more and more withdrawn as the days passed, grieving over David, longing to be with him, and anxious simply to make contact with him. She had had no opportunity to reach him by phone since she had arrived back home to hell the day that Cassie had made the one phone call that had literally sent Sara's life into a downward spiral.

The devastating aftermath, yet to unfold, would resonate through the rest of Sara's life. Cassie's few words to Sara's daddy by phone would soon prove Proverbs 18:21, "The tongue has the power of life and death."

In constant companion with fear of her daddy and fear of the entire world around her, Sara's thoughts were consumed with how she might possibly escape him. David was her answer. She felt confident that David truly loved her and could rescue her. She tried to sneak phone calls to him from the one telephone in their house, stationed at the massive desk that crowded her parent's bedroom. But her daddy caught her in several attempts, and she lied her way out of the likely threat of physical punishment.

Over several weeks, she would quietly slip out of her Sunday morning Sunday School class at church, as if she were going to the restroom. Knowing her daddy was occupied in his own class, she would make phone connection with David. She'd move into the dark, unoccupied office near her classroom, silently close the door behind her where no one could see or hear her, and use the telephone. Through her stolen phone conversations with David, his love and concern for her was confirmed. He was concerned for her safety and wanted nothing more than to steal her away where he could protect her and give her a happy life.

After a time, during those weekly, stolen moments over the phone, their plan was in place. A specific day and time was confirmed for her that they would run off together. She would be free—and freely in the arms of the man she loved!

It was early summer. Sara had just completed her junior year of high school and, of course, no longer had a job. She was only allowed out of the house with her mama or daddy in company—to go to church or to the store. There was no easy escape and very little alone time. Her mama had been instructed by her husband to not let Sara out of her sight while he was away at work. There was only one viable option for her escape.

David and Sara planned that she would pack a small bag, late on Saturday night, and during the Sunday School hour at church the next morning she would leave the church building and walk the couple of blocks out of sight of the church to the designated place where David would be waiting. They would then drive to her house, grab her hidden bag and leave, for good. They would disappear—her parents, her siblings, her friends, none the wiser.

Sara had not thought through the complications and ramifications that were facing David. He was grown man; she was a minor. Had he considered his daughter? His job? His extended family and friends? What about the fact that he would, in essence, be kidnapping a young woman—a child—and likely be prosecuted for statutory rape and kidnapping? None of these things entered Sara's self-absorbed, immature mind. Her sole intent was to get out at any cost and be with the man she loved.

She was ready on that Sunday morning. Fear gripped her mind and body over the monumental and dangerous thing she was attempting. Nevertheless, her desperate love for David, coupled with her desperate desire to escape her daddy, drove Sara to act beyond her fears and carry out their plans.

On that blinding and humid Sunday morning in early June, 1976, she quietly slipped out of her classroom and quickly exited the church while everyone was diverted by their Sunday School studies. Her heart pounded wildly. Her stomach was upset over the sheer nerve of what she was doing, interwoven with anxiety that her daddy might catch her in the act. She knew how dangerous this plan was in light of her daddy's control, rage, and relentlessness. If he caught her on the run, she knew he would kill David for certain this time, and most assuredly lock her away in hell forever and throw away the keys, if not beat her to death.

Sara's daddy was merciless in his expectations and control over his family and in the punishments he administered. He would surely go completely berserk if he discovered her in the midst of running away. But this plan was her only hope to escape him for good and be in the arms of someone who truly loved her and found value in her. It was worth the life risk she was taking.

She was tied up in knots and shaking, barely able to walk as she quickly and quietly abandoned all that she knew and headed toward freedom. She peered back over her shoulder from time to time as she made her way out the back door of the church and across the vast, open, asphalt lot until she had safely rounded the first corner, out of sight. Heart pounding through her chest and her breathing labored with anxiety and anticipation, she made her way up the hill, past the four-story, seedy apartment building hugging the backside of a rundown strip mall, and left at the next corner. Their church was located in a poor and unsafe area of town. Alone on the streets in that neighborhood was dangerous enough for a petite and pretty young woman, but again, worth the risk to Sara. She was almost there. Freedom was now only a few steps away, the moment she had longed and prayed for her entire life.

When she reached the designated place, David wasn't there. She looked around in a panic, a myriad of questions and thoughts raced through her mind like a freight train. She waited; she watched nervously every vehicle that approached, keeping a desperate eye on the road for David's truck. She was certain her daddy would discover her missing and find her on the street corner, two blocks away, waiting to run away with David. The longer she waited the more anxious, devastated, and panicked she became. Time was critical; time was running out. Sunday school was only an hour long. Her parents would expect to see her sitting in the pew next to them, along with her siblings, when the preaching service began. She either had to escape *now*, with David, or quickly get back to the church building before she was discovered missing. She otherwise had no place to go, no place to run.

The questions and fears swirled in her head as she continued to wait, hope, and pray that David would show up. *Where is he? Why isn't he here?* She cried. *Doesn't he love me? Is he afraid?* The questions surged through her head as she panicked. How would she survive if she had to return to the church, her life, and hell under her daddy's skewed and demented authority?

As the minutes ticked away, she knew in her heart that David wasn't going to come, or he would have been there already. She reconciled that she had no choice but to get back to the church before she was discovered missing, or her daddy saw her walking toward the church from some distant place. She would never be able to explain where she had been, or what she had been up to. He would know that she had snuck out to meet David.

There was no time left. She knew she could wait no longer for David. He simply wasn't coming after all. Her heart bled in despair, desperation, and grief. She wanted nothing more than to die, right then and there. All her hopes were once again destroyed. There was no one in whom she could trust or depend. *No one.* She had not only been emotionally abandoned all of her life by her daddy, abandoned from protection by her mama, her relatives, her teachers, other parents, and her church, but now abandoned by the man she truly believed loved her. As scary as death was, she would have welcomed the ultimate escape by suicide. But to what end? Eternity was a long, long time—without end—forever and ever. How could she take that ultimate risk which would forever seal her fate to eternal hopelessness and darkness by killing herself? Surely this would be the outcome to taking one's own life. *Wouldn't it?* She wasn't certain.

She knew, as she sprinted back to the church carrying a heavy burden of grief and despair, that she could not be seen crying when she reentered the building. She had to have herself pulled together, her emotions held intact. She was good at pushing down the pain, the hurt, the anger...but tears stormed inside her. She had learned to be a seasoned actor for the sake of survival.

She entered the building, silently screaming and weeping. Sunday school was just letting out and folks were making their way to the sanctuary. No one she passed along the corridors or in the sanctuary knew of the turmoil, grief, and defeat she held tightly within her, like holding back the reigns of wild horses raging to break free.

Chapter Ten

In the ensuing days, Sara was able to sneak opportunities here and there to make telephone contact with David. She desperately loved him and grieved her loss of him a second time, and her hope of freedom that was snatched away in a matter of twenty minutes when he had not shown up to take her away.

Her first conversation with him in the aftermath was in anguish and confusion over why he had not been there, why he had not kept his word and picked her up the previous Sunday morning as planned.

"Where were you?!" She cried, trying to hold back her tears. "What happened?!"

"I'm so sorry, Baby Doll," he breathed with regret. "I love you and had every intention of taking you away, but when the time came, I just couldn't take that enormous risk."

A heavy fog of silence hung in the air as Sara's mind raced, trying to formulate the risks in her grieving mind and weigh them against her love for David and her desire to be free to love him, and to escape her daddy for good.

"My daughter…," he trailed off. "I don't know what I was thinking, Sara. If you and I ran away together, we would have to leave the state and hide from everyone we know until you turn eighteen. I would not be there for my daughter. I love her, too. She's only a baby and needs her daddy. I can't leave her or risk destroying three lives," he reasoned quietly.

This struck a deep place within Sara. She needed him, too. She had also needed her own daddy, but he had never been there for her, and certainly not with the love and protection that David gave to his daughter. She quietly wept with the weight of grief over losing David again, and over never having had a daddy who loved her. There were no words to counter his, no words to ease the pain or loss.

"You're underage, Sara—a minor. There would be an APB out for both of us, all over the state, naming me a kidnapper. That's a federal offense," he gently reminded. This is serious stuff. I'm so sorry I've let you down," he offered in sincerity and defeat.

David could hear her quiet tears and imagined them streaking her youthful face, her dark mascara mixed with the darkness of hurt, confusion, grief, and resignation. He hated himself and wanted to reach through the phone and hold her, comfort her. "Baby Doll, please don't cry," he pleaded. "Everything will be okay in time, you'll see. This is just temporary. You'll be eighteen this time next year and we can be together," he encouraged. "It won't be long."

Ultimately, David had had to consider *real* life, not a fairytale that would never exist. He knew better, but had not wanted to face the truth. He loved Sara and wanted to have a real life with her, but he had also wanted the best for her. In the end, he knew he had to do the right thing for her, for himself, and for his daughter.

She feared she would never again be able to see him and that he would go on with his life—without her. How could she live without him and continue to live with her daddy, a man she hated, feared, and distrusted? Life was simply not worth living. She wanted to lay down her life as she laid down the telephone.

♥ ♥ ♥

Sara was lost and alone. She was deeply depressed and despondent in the weeks that followed. In addition, it became more and more apparent that her daddy could not—would not—let go of what he imagined she and David had done together sexually. Sara didn't know or understand at the time that her own daddy was out of his head with jealousy. He continued to demand that she tell him how David had touched her and what they had done together.

Sara continued to deny everything he suggested. Every day was a grave, emotional struggle and a deep, tormenting heartache for Sara. She was physically ill and exhausted with extraordinarily overwrought emotions.

Watching Sara's physical and emotional demise and how she apparently would not let go of her thoughts and longing to be with David, her parents made the decision to send her off with a small group from their church who were taking their annual, summer mission trip to southern Mexico. As always, the group would be led by "the preacher" and his wife. Sara couldn't believe her daddy was actually sending her away for two weeks—and so far—to a foreign country. She had hardly been anywhere outside her state, much less out of the country, and now she was going down to the Guatemalan border—*without* her family! She envisioned the reprieve and freedom from her daddy. This would be the longest she had ever been away from him.

She also envisioned all the opportunities she would have to make phone calls to David during her two-week probation from hell, called "home." It had never been a true home, but rather a house of imprisonment, torture, and terror. In spite of her deep depression, the very thought of escaping her daddy for two whole weeks, and the rare opportunity to experience another culture, evoked excitement in her. She could hardly wait for the trip, although her first choice would have been a permanent trip—with David.

Southern Mexico was an eye-opening experience that Sara would never forget. It fostered in her an even deeper compassion for others, especially those less fortunate. She witnessed how very poorly the people lived throughout the southern villages, apart from the large cities. Families lived in tiny, open, stucco huts. She ate with a family whose hut, like all the others, had dirt floors, open doors and windows without glass or screening. The outdoor bathroom was just outside their open kitchen where family animals freely roamed in and out—goats, dogs, chickens. Despite poor living conditions—according to American standards—they were a happy, generous people. Astounding!

What most impressed Sara was how people with so little could be so generous and eager to share their meager provisions with foreigners. She was completely amazed by the people, their attitudes, culture, food, scenery.

With her temporary parole and drastic change of environment, Sara began to regain some of her will to live and to hold on to the hope that she would someday escape her daddy—and hopefully re-connect with David. As best as she could, through very poor phone connections and a language barrier, Sara attempted to contact David throughout the two weeks. Just hearing his voice fed her and encouraged her toward a future.

Sara hated the thought of returning home to her daddy. She grew more and more depressed as they took the long drive back up through the southern states, heading northeast toward home. She had no clue what her future might hold, only that it was the immediate future she wanted to run from—going back home.

When she re-entered her house, she had no idea how her world was about to be shaken to her very core, as it had never before been shaken, nor how this pivotal point in her life would dynamically reshape her from the inside out and plunge her toward a living hell beyond all she had endured already, and near death.

Upon returning home to the reality of such a strict environment, she was again resigned to the likelihood that she and David would never be together. Nevertheless, she continued to take every opportunity to contact him. Her daddy constantly monitored her every move and caught her in several attempts to reach David. Each time, she adamantly lied to him about who she had been calling, and he couldn't prove otherwise.

Lying had become a safety net for her. He had taught her and proved to her through the years that she could not trust him with her safety or care, and therefore her honesty. Her honesty with him had always resulted in injury and terror. She had learned to lie to protect herself and survive. Lying was the only thing she knew to ensure her safety.

❤ ❤ ❤

It wasn't long after Sara's return home from Mexico that her daddy began to make sexual remarks to her—quietly, out of earshot of her mama—about how she looked or how her clothes looked on her. Her blood ran cold with fear and hot with hatred. The same sick feeling arose in her that she had had as a budding young teen when he had come into her room several nights under the pretense of wanting to rub her back, but this was so much more sickening because he was no longer subtle. Now, without reserve or dignity, he openly scanned her body with lustful eyes and made quiet, sickening remarks to her about how her clothes conformed to her body.

She was repulsed and sickened to the point of despair. She wanted to kill him and run as far away as she could. Evil hung in the air like a thick, hot, smothering blanket suffocating her. Sara despised him. His blatant behavior took Sara's horror to a whole new level. She would far rather be beaten by him to her death than see the way he openly measured her tiny body and hear his sexual remarks.

She prayed and prayed in desperation to escape somehow, but there was no place to go, no one to tell. All she had to cling to was her sheer faith and hope in God that He would somehow make a way for her permanent escape. If only she were brave enough to run away. The outside world was far too foreign and scary as well, and she had no place to go. How would she survive any better outside those walls of terror, alone in a big and scary world? How would she eat? Where would she sleep? If her own biological daddy would be so terrifying, merciless, and untrustworthy toward her, how might a stranger treat her if she were picked up along the road?! There was no where to turn, no place to run, no place to hide, no one to trust.

The unknown was equally as scary as the familiar horrors she had known for sixteen years. No matter how bad, it was the only home and only way of life she had ever known. At least she had food and a roof over her head, and she had the love and companionship of her four siblings and her mama. But still, she lived in terror of him.

She prayed and hoped that she would live to see adulthood when she could somehow, finally, be free of him. She prayed and wept ceaselessly as she lay on her bed each night, looking out at the stars, believing God was out there watching over her and hearing her pleas.

On the weekends or evenings, whenever Sara's daddy would go somewhere—the grocery store, the hardware store, the automotive store—he would have Sara go with him, alone. He even insisted she go with him whenever he had to take a day trip out of town for his job. Not long after they'd take off in the car, he'd tell Sara to scoot over next to him, as if she was his girlfriend. Sara detested him all the more, repulsed at his sick, overt sexual behavior toward his own daughter, and that she had to keep it all stuffed inside out of fear of him. She detested him and the love songs he would sing to her as they traveled. The cancer of hatred and the inferno hot and festering rage churning deep within her was continually fed every time he demanded her attention in an inappropriate way. Each time he'd talk to her, sing to her, and look at her with open lust, she'd die a little more inside and want to *kill* him.

Chapter Eleven

Near the end of summer, as Sara approached her senior year of high school, his obsession with her had grown so apparent that even her siblings took notice and, strangely enough, were jealous—certainly not because they cared for him (they didn't!), but from the basic, human need to be loved and valued by a parent. They didn't see or know the hell she was living. They only saw that he was paying special attention to her. From their skewed and unknowledgeable perspective, it appeared to them that Sara had become their daddy's star student, his favorite child, overnight. Weighted down by a heavy blanket of fear, she simply didn't have the courage to tell them what was really going on, how sick, terrified, and totally reviled she was at the very sight of him.

Her mama saw the changes in his attitude toward Sara,

as well. She saw that Sara was withdrawing more and more and becoming increasingly more touchy and ill-tempered. What she saw happening between her husband and daughter infused in her suspicion, mistrust, and a growing anger toward her husband that she suppressed. It was far easier and safer for her to keep peace and not interfere, so she did nothing to help her daughter. She had never overtly done anything to protect her daughter. She was too intimidated by her husband to confront him about the time he was spending with Sara each night and his uncommon attention to her.

One morning, Sara heard her daddy say the words that would send her spiraling into the depths of despair and a hell she could not imagine surviving. Her end had come.

It was a bright Sunday morning in late August. Sara—like the rest of the family—was getting ready for church. As teenagers, she and Allie had shared their parent's dresser mirror with their mama, to apply makeup and do their hair. The house was so small, and the single bathroom always occupied, it had become habit for the three of them to primp in front of the lengthy mirror. Today was no different, except that Allie had just recently departed for college, and her mama was in the kitchen preparing breakfast. Sara was alone in her parent's room, in front of the mirror.

She was jealous that Allie had been able to escape, but it gave her hope that she could use college as her way out, too. Her daddy had finally relented and allowed Allie to go away to school, gently but persistently persuaded by Allie and her mama. Their mama had always been a huge advocate of education and had spent much time working with her children through the years to teach them, in addition to what they gained at school. Especially in English, grammar, and reading. A southern accent was heritage, but poor grammar added to it, perpetuating the hillbilly stereotype, was unacceptable to their mama. She was constantly correcting their improper use of language. She also told them quietly and often that they could be anything they wanted to be if they went to college, and set their mind to their dreams. "Where there's a will, there's a way," she often quoted.

Allowing Allie to move out to go to school was a huge concession for him, but not without condition. She could only go if she attended the fundamental seminary supported by their church. Allie didn't care where—or even if—she went to school; she only cared, as Sara did, that she find a way to escape their daddy—and never return.

Sara was brushing her lengthy, thick hair when he entered his bedroom. He stopped very close to her, bent down to her ear and quietly whispered, so no one else might hear, "I'm going to do to you everything that man did to you."

His words were like a bomb shell exploding inside of Sara, and the greatest terror and dread she had ever known seized her. She couldn't say a word; she was paralyzed by the magnitude and impact of his clear intentions. In that moment, Sara began to pray vehemently for death. She prayed to die, and she prayed for him to die. Her fear intermingled with her fierce hatred of him, a hatred that would grow and deepen with his every look, his every word, and his every touch. Her childhood prayer would have cried out a little differently, "Now I lay me down to sleep." She trembled. "I pray the Lord my soul to keep. *Please let me die before I wake*," she pleaded. "I pray the Lord my soul to take."

The family attended Sunday school that morning as usual, followed by the morning preaching service. They stayed after church, throughout the afternoon, while their daddy did his volunteer work for the preacher. The hours dragged on, Sara's mind was consumed with turmoil and panic over the inevitable, vile betrayal that her own daddy was planning against her. He always followed through with whatever he said he was going to do to his children—*always*. He had proven that fact to her without exception for sixteen years. Now, instead of ravaging her naked body with his belt, he was going to *rape* her! She was desperate, crazed in her mind, and frozen with a terror unlike she had ever been at his evil, insane hand; and he *whistled* through the day at church— like a saint—all the while entertaining himself with his perverse intentions against her! He was truly the real Jekyll and Hyde. He was truly insane, a madman, the ultimate hypocrite, the undeniable Judas, *the devil himself*—and no one was the wiser to this most hideous scheme, except Sara.

Inside, her mental and emotional world was chaos, and her life appeared to quickly be coming to a devastating and horrific end; but outside, around her, everything played out as usual, and at a sickeningly slow pace. The afternoon segued into the evening church activities, her mind in a whirlwind of desperation. There was choir practice at 5:00 p.m., followed by the 6:00 p.m. DTU—Doctrinal Training Union classes. The usual smiles and bantering of the large church family swirled around her before settling in for the 7:00 p.m. preaching service, but there was no one—*no one*—she could tell. Terror screamed inside her.

Each hour drew her closer to burning alive at the stake

by his evil, premeditated plan of sexual violation against her, and there was nothing, and no one, to stop him. There was no place for her to run, no place to hide, no one to tell. She was trapped in a living nightmare, in evil's vice grip, the devil himself—her own daddy—crushing her, and no one else knew. He made it all the more sickening and evil when he also whistled and hummed his favorite hymns on the long drive home to a very real hell—her hell. He was truly a living *monster*.

That night, after their usual "Daily Bible Readings," he stayed up after everyone else had gone to bed. He quietly visited Sara's room and summoned her into the living room. He sat on "his" sofa chair like a king on his throne. Sara stood before him, her tiny but fully developed sixteen-year-old body a mere four foot, eleven inches, and eighty-six pounds. Every ounce of her was shaking with fear, dread, and hatred. She was face to face with a real-life monster.

He commanded her to unbutton her pajama top so he could look at her body. Terrified and panicked, she tearfully pleaded with him, "Please, please, no …"

She was clothed only with the heaviest shame and humiliation when he proceeded to touch her, rape her and rob her of her most intimate self, her innocence, her dignity, and what little was left of her childhood. In that hour of her greatest anguish, *he sealed within her that she was worth nothing*, and left her only with the greatest, deepest, all-consuming hatred and a death sentence.

The hatred and injustice burned inside her and filled every fiber of her being. She pleaded with him again, "Please, no … this is wrong!"

His reply stunned her. "Do you think after God leading me all these years that He would lead me wrong in this?"

Shocked beyond all belief by his insanity, she realized just how mentally ill a man he truly was. But the full reality of his perversity and obsession settled like a concrete mass in her heart when he continued, "The day you were born, I knew you were my gift from God. Your body is mine, your mind is mine, and your soul is mine, to do with as I please."

In that moment, Sara's entire life became much clearer to her, like a veil had been lifted from her eyes. She realized that her *entire* life had been built on that inconceivable lie from the pit of hell. You see, Sara was born on Father's Day. It shocked and horrified her to realize that simply because she had been born *on* Father's Day, her daddy, in his demented, disturbed, and evil-possessed mind, truly believed she was his personal possession from God, to do with as he pleased. Her entire life had been built on that foundation of possession, obsession, and determination to totally make her his own—first by breaking her spirit and molding her mind to his will through extensive fear and physical abuse, then by taking her body in the most cruel, robbing, and intimate way.

The sexual molestation continued night after night. Sara was dying an agonizing emotional death that can only be fully understood by those who have been sexually abused. Through the days of that hell week, while her daddy was at work, Sara was unable to do anything except weep and pray, and search the scriptures for *something* to hang on to. She was at the end of her rope, at the end of hope. She was physically ill and emotionally spent. At sixteen, she was done.

While many of her peers were enjoying the summer and looking forward to their senior year of high school and planning their futures, Sara's only thoughts were how she was going to kill herself or kill her daddy, though neither choice offered her freedom or hope. Sara lay in her bed sobbing, and weighed the cost of suicide versus murder. It had come down to a matter of life and death.

Sara reasoned. *I could slit my wrists in the bathtub, with the door locked so no one would see me or rescue me before I was dead. But, slicing my skin open would really hurt,* she backtracked. *How could I cut myself open with a sharp knife without severe pain?* She knew that would be impossible, that it would hurt really badly. She wanted to die, but without pain. She had had too much physical pain in her life and was terrified of more. Though she regularly inflicted pain on herself out of anxiety, it would be altogether different to cut her flesh open with a sharp knife, and see her blood spurting out, filling the tub.

I would be the second person to die in that bathtub. Her thoughts segued to drowning. Her phobia quickly eliminated that option.

The easiest and painless way would be to take a bottle of pills, she concluded. *But if I kill myself, will I go to hell or heaven?* How could she know for certain? She had been rightly taught by her church that God alone was the author of life and death, and that death was a divine decision of God where no man was to tread. She didn't recall the preacher or her Sunday School teachers ever saying that a person would go to hell if they committed suicide, but it was implied. It was also implied that if a person took his own life, he was not likely "saved" in the first place.

To take her own life and take that irreversible decision from God sounded unforgivable to Sara. She wasn't 100% certain. She didn't think there was anyone she could ask who really knew the truth. There was a 50/50 chance of going to heaven (or hell), to her way of thinking. It was too big a risk to take, knowing that eternity was forever and ever. She was certain that she would go to one or the other, though. She didn't believe in an in-between, a holding place for the dead. She knew the scriptures well enough to know there was nothing Biblical to support that theory, and she believed God's Word alone. It was just too risky a gamble to take her own life.

But why should I be the one to die and not him? She converted her thinking out of desperation. *He's the one who's evil. He's the one who hurts everybody. He should die! He doesn't deserve to take another breath.* She didn't consider that murder would also be taking the decision of life and death out of God's hands; but she did consider what the Bible clearly says about murder. She was well versed in the Ten Commandments. There was no misunderstanding Exodus 20:13 (KJV), "Thou shalt not kill." She had no questions in this regard. However, she didn't consider that "Thou shalt not kill" also meant taking one's own life. She had always had the mindset that this commandment meant taking the life of another person.

Though she had heard from the pulpit, all of her life, "Once saved, always saved," *surely there would be dire, eternal consequences for murdering my daddy*, she surmised. She wasn't altogether confident that she would not be cast into eternal flames for breaking that commandment, "saved" or not. She just didn't know the truth. Plus, if she killed her daddy, she would most surely go straight to a different kind of prison, where she would have to live out the rest of her life in a different earthly hell—the penitentiary. She had heard horror stories about how prisoners physically mistreated and raped the less powerful. She shuddered as that terror gripped her. She would not even consider exchanging one kind of hell for another. She was seeking *freedom*.

Neither choice—suicide or murder—brought hope of true freedom. There was no good way to end this living nightmare that consumed, imprisoned, and tortured her. All that remained in her was the hope and faith that God would deliver her—by death or escape. What other alternative did she have except to choose life and survive by her sheer hope in God that she would someday have a future? *God* was the only answer. So, she kept on praying, hoping, weeping, and pouring through the pages of the Word of Life.

You must be wondering (with the family living in such close quarters), where Sara's mama was night after night during that hell week of molestation, incest. She was there, hidden away in her bedroom, too intimidated and afraid of her husband to confront him and protect her daughter. She felt helpless to intervene. While she was not absolutely certain what was going on in their living room late at night between her husband and daughter, she had a very good suspicion, evidenced by Sara's physical and emotional decline.

Finally, Sara's mama could take it no more. She mustered up the courage to gingerly question him about keeping their daughter up so late at night, and what they were doing. Hesitantly she suggested to him, "You know, Sara needs her sleep." Then, after a moment of stalling, she bravely but timidly followed in a casual tone, "What are ya'll doing up so late at night in the living room?"

In true character, he lashed back in his authoritative, manipulative way, "Can't I spend any time alone with my daughter?"

As usual, Sara's mama backed down, her fear and intimidation outweighing the inherent instinct to rise up and protect her babies from harm. She wanted to intervene, to know what was going on in their living room each night. She wanted to put her suspicions to rest, but she felt debilitated from taking action. She would have to work up more courage to confront him further, if he continued to keep Sara up with him at night.

She watched Sara move about like a zombie during the day, alternately sobbing and sick to her stomach, unable to eat and eventually unable to do anything but lay on her bed and weep. Out of fear, Sara would draw up all the energy within her to feign "normal" in the evenings when her daddy arrived home from work, but she had little energy left and no desire to live. Sara's starkly contrasting behaviors between day and night congealed her mama's suspicions. She knew something was terribly wrong and could only imagine what her husband must be doing to their daughter every night. The God-created, inborn need to protect her child *finally* awoke in her mama. She could no longer stand by and do nothing.

The next morning, after her husband left for work, she got her two older boys, Matt and John, off on their scheduled Boy Scout outing, and Wayne, her youngest, occupied outside in play. She went into the children's room and sat on the edge of Allie's bed, adjacent to Sara lying on her bed, sobbing, and said, "You have to tell me what's going on."

Sara couldn't believe her ears. Was her mama truly coming to her rescue? Sara quickly grew even more terrified because her daddy had told her that if her mama knew what was going on, her mama would have a nervous breakdown and end up in the hospital.

The evil one, Satan, not only lies and deceives and manipulates but knows our greatest weakness, and this becomes his direct target to keep us in bondage and fear. Sara's weakness had always been her mama. She had a deep compassion and love for her mama, even though her mama had never protected her.

Sara knew how much her mama loved her, and she also recognized the debilitating power of fear and intimidation that Sara's daddy had over her mama. She loved her mama so deeply and compassionately, the thought of her mama going away to a hospital meant losing the only parental love she had. In addition, if her mama went away, Sara would truly be left alone in that hell house with that monster, giving him even more freedom to do with Sara whatever he willed. She couldn't bear the thought of either. In her young mind, the potential cost was far too great to risk telling her mama what he was doing to her each night.

Her mama pleaded with her, "Please tell me what's going on. I can't help you if you don't tell me."

Further hope sprang up in Sara's heart. *Will she really help me?* Would her mama really rise up for the first time and protect Sara and help her to escape? Was it possible? Her mind swirled with a mixture of doubt, hope, anxiety, and great fear as she continued to sob. She replied, "I can't. I can't tell you."

Her mama continued to plead with her, "I believe I know what's going on, but I have to hear it from you. Please tell me."

The hope that her mama might truly know what he was doing to her every night, coupled with her mama's pleas to tell her, bolstered in Sara the courage and trust she needed to uncover the truth and expose him for the perverted man he was. She desperately needed help to escape him. This was her only chance, her only opportunity, her only hope. With fear and trepidation, she told her mama how he was molesting her each night.

Sickened at hearing what she had feared to be true, her mama gravely replied, "That's what I thought." Then, with unprecedented determination and authority in her voice she said, "Pack your clothes. I'm taking you away right now."

A million diverse thoughts raced through Sara's head, fueled by an all-consuming fear that made it difficult for her to breathe or feel her own body moving as she quickly began to pack her clothes, sobbing, and forcing back the bile rising in her throat. She was desperately afraid. Like a crazed animal she raced about, gathering up as many of her things as she could, feeling as though her daddy would walk into the house at any moment and discover their attempt to flee. She was convinced, in her traumatized state of mind, that he would somehow clairvoyantly know what they were doing. After all, he had told her that he could leave his body and "fly," so it wasn't beyond her imagination that he could possess the supernatural ability to know what was happening at

NOW I LAY ME DOWN TO SLEEP: THE STORY OF SARA

home. She was certain he would arrive home at any moment and intercede before they could get out.

As quickly as possible, Sara's mama put her and Wayne in the car and drove the thirty minutes to their church. She needed to seek counsel from "the preacher" as to what she should do—where she should take Sara.

Behind closed doors, Sara's mama told him what Sara had shared with her. Sara sat next to her mama on the matching, cold leather chair facing the preacher's massive mahogany desk. She was humiliated and in a hysterical state of frenzy, gripped with fear and weeping uncontrollably. She was certain that it was only a matter of time before her daddy would get wind of what her mama was doing and come after them. He would surely kill them both—surely. He was a madman.

So many things about her daddy's mental, emotional, and spiritual state had become clear to her during those five nights she'd spent imprisoned at his hand. Added to his sick obsession over her, she was now, more than ever, inclined to believe he was possessed by an evil spirit—a spirit that would indeed give him psychic knowledge that would propel him to come after her. The depth of fear that consumed Sara devastated her mind and emotions, as well as her body.

She heard the preacher tell her mama that she should take Sara away right then, to some distant place where she would be safe, and where her daddy would not know where she was or easily be able to get to her.

"I could take her to my sister's house in the next state," her mama considered aloud. She knew her sister, Aggie, and brother-in-law, Perin, would take good care of Sara, and they were two hours away. *It would be harder for him to get to Sara,* she convinced herself.

"That sounds like the best plan." The preacher chimed in. "Take her straight away and don't tell anyone where you've taken her," he added with authority.

Two hours later, they crossed the state line, headed for Sara's favorite aunt and uncle's home. Sara deeply loved Aunt Aggie and Uncle P. (as the nieces and nephews called him), with much affection. They loved Sara just as deeply and would do anything in the world for the children and their mama. Sara's mama was the baby of her family and just a young child when her two older sisters married. They had always made themselves available to her and the children, opening their homes and hearts without reserve, knowing how strict and difficult Sara's daddy was.

As the three traveled, Sara continued to sob out of a desperate, all-consuming fear. She constantly looked over her shoulder, out the back window, convinced she would see her daddy racing up the highway behind them at any moment. She imagined all sorts of confrontations that would end in her and her mama's defeat. Wayne, only eight years old, was uncharacteristically subdued, frightened, not understanding what was happening, or why his beloved big sister was so terribly upset. He loved her so ... he hated to see her crying and so afraid. It made him afraid, too. He bristled up in his seat, angry that someone had caused such upset in his sister, and eager to plow them. He had proven in the past to be feisty with protection when one of her older brothers would hurt or threaten her as siblings do.

By the time they arrived at Aunt Aggie and Uncle P.'s

house, Sara was unable to function due to the emotional, mental, and physical toll the fear and sexual molestation had taken on her. She was still convinced that her daddy knew where she was and that he would come after her.

Her mama, aunt, and uncle discussed all that had transpired and the best plan to care for Sara. While they talked, she was consumed with thoughts of her daddy appearing outside one of the windows and peering in at her with his alien-like eyes. His confession to her about his astral traveling had convinced her that he was capable of almost anything—the supernatural no exception.

She was so out of her mind with terror that she could not be left alone for even a minute. She couldn't even go to the bathroom alone or sleep alone. That night, her mama slept with her. Sara lay huddled under the covers close to her mama, her eyes staring wide toward the window, too afraid to fall asleep. But the next day, her mama had to leave. She had two other children at home to care for, and she had to deal with Sara's daddy. She left Sara behind, secure in the love and care she knew her sister and brother-in-law would give. Sara was still so traumatized that night, and for several after, that her aunt slept next to her. With the passing of time, she would become more at ease that her daddy was not going to appear and try to force her back home.

Her mama had telephoned him the evening they arrived at her sister's. She knew he would be home from work at 5:30 p.m. to find them gone. With unprecedented courage, fueled by anger—and regret that she had not intervened sooner—she told him she knew what he had been doing to their daughter and that she had taken Sara away. She told him she wanted him out of the house by the next day, before she got back home, and to take *his chair* with him. She also informed him that she had gone to the preacher that morning and that he had advised her to take Sara away. Suddenly, Sara's daddy had fallen from his righteous position in the eyes of the church, as well as his lofty place as self-appointed king over his family. He knew he had no choice but to move out as she had demanded. He'd been caught, and many eyes were now on him.

Sara had been equally surprised and relieved when she learned that her mama had demanded that he move out. Sara could hardly believe that her mama had had the guts to finally confront him after so many years of doing nothing, and had taken action to save Sara and her siblings.

Why, oh why, had it taken so long? Why had no one in Sara's life intervened until it had escalated to the point of life and death? Where had her relatives been, her school teachers and Sunday School teachers? Where had the parents of her church friends been? Was it all so well hidden that no one seemed to know? Or was it just too socially taboo to talk about or to intervene on behalf of the safety and well-being of a child? Was her lifelong nightmare truly over? Was he finally out of their lives forever?

He moved out that evening to his mother's home across town, but not before making a quick attempt to do something heroic to save himself in the eyes of his wife and the church. Matt and John had just arrived home from their scouting trip and found him crying. He insisted they all three get down on their knees and the two boys pray to be saved. Neither of his boys said a word. They were scared, sensing that something terrible had happened. Their mama was nowhere in sight, nor Wayne or Sara.

At age fifteen, Matt suspected correctly that all of this had something to do with Sara and why she had been so distraught throughout the entire week, and his daddy had been spending an awful lot of time alone with her, and taking her places with him. He quickly put the two facts together as they were down on their knees, and figured that his daddy was trying to make some kind of restitution to his mama by getting his boys saved.

Neither boy uttered a word as he continued to insist that they pray to be saved. John was too young to have a clue what all the crying and urgency was about; he was only eleven. But Matt had accurately assessed what was happening and wasn't about to give his cruel and two-faced daddy the satisfaction of using him and his little brother to gloat to their mama about how he had gotten the boys saved. Matt despised him all the more.

In later years, Sara would come to understand how those who are abused become abusers, and would suspect that her daddy had been abused in some form as a child. And she would learn about generational curses that must be broken. She knew a little bit of his history, but she could never get a straight answer out of his sister in regard to abuse when Sara had attempted to research her suspicions. She knew one thing for certain: her daddy had the same irritated and easily angered attitude toward his mother that Sara felt toward him. This in itself was suspect, that he had likely been abused as a child. But she would also come to understand that while abusers become abusers by no fault of their own, abusers *stay* abusers by *choice*. She would come to know that regardless of whether or not he had been abused as a child, he had made conscious, adult choices *again and again* to abuse his children and have no regard or mercy for their suffering or well-being. No matter his own childhood, Sara knew his adult choices were inexcusable.

♥ ♥ ♥

A few weeks after her mama had left her at Aunt Aggie's and Uncle P.'s, Sara began to gradually feel more safe in her new environment, so they felt comfortable to enroll her in the private, Protestant school nearby where she could begin her senior year of high school, but still be close to their home. They were ever watchful and careful of her safety, knowing that her daddy might turn up at any moment and take her. Although she was still fearful that her daddy would show up one day, she began to relax somewhat and began to blossom in her new life of freedom.

Aunt Aggie and Uncle P. nurtured her, protected her, and loved her along the journey toward healing and a renewed life. They were a Godsend. They were the kind of caregivers that God had intended parents to be. They were Jesus to her— feeding, clothing, sheltering, and loving her unconditionally, without hesitation or reserve. They, and her mama, had truly saved Sara's life and probably never knew at the time just how critical a truth this was. No one had known all that Sara had been contemplating in her heart and mind toward suicide and murder, and how close she had come to both.

She quickly made friends at school. Just as quickly, she landed the position as pianist for the school's weekly church service assembly, which all the students attended. She felt really proud and appreciated for the very first time on stage. All the years prior, her performing experiences had been laden with fear and distress. There was no allowance for appreciation or healthy pride. It was a new freedom that gave her more confidence and encouraged her to share her musical talents.

Very little bothered or upset her now—she was so exuberant in her freedom from consuming fear, anxiety, her daddy, and the past. The little things that upset her peers were inconsequential to Sara because "normal" was so new and refreshing—a true blessing.

She recognized that boys were noticing her and flirting with her, but she was surprised when several began to ask her out. Inside, she still felt like a little kid, rather than a high school senior. She didn't know herself at all. She had no confidence. She didn't understand the world around her or how to interact and be a part of normalcy. Although she had been raised in public schools, she hadn't been allowed to be involved in the social aspects as she was now. So, she didn't know how she was supposed to act, interact, or respond to the boys who vied for her attention and affection. Dating and having male friends had never been an option for her—until now.

She had been firmly conditioned by her daddy to do nothing outside his permission or will, or outside the rules laid down by their church, most especially where it pertained to the opposite sex. She was completely lost when it came to interacting with boys in a natural way toward dating. Aunt Aggie and Uncle P. were very lovingly protective of Sara— completely unlike what she was accustomed to—and gently cautioned her against spending too much time and focus on boys beyond mere friendships. They were aware, to a degree, of all she had suffered and didn't want to see her experience further heartache, upset, and trauma that is a natural part of high school romances. They gave her the freedom to date, and encouraged her friendships, under their kind and gentle guidance, but she simply didn't know what to do with herself in this regard. She was like a new colt trying to run and play for the first time and felt just as gangly in her relationships.

Eventually, Sara settled into a pleasant and peaceful routine, little by little feeling more secure in her new surroundings and lifestyle, but it was short lived.

One Saturday, three months into her senior year, Sara's mama called her with disturbing news. "Sara," her mama hesitated, "I've let your daddy move back home." Silence. Sara was stunned at what she was hearing. "He says he's changed," her mama offered quietly. "And I really believe he has."

Changed?! Sara knew he had visited a psychiatrist at the insistence of their preacher, but only one time. *Was her mama crazy?* "Mother!" She cried in horror. "How could he have *possibly* changed after only *one* visit to a psychiatrist?" She screamed at her mama in disbelief. She was stunned and shaken and thought her mama had completely lost all her sensibilities. *Why... how could she allow him to re-enter their lives after all they had suffered under his rule?* She knew well that her daddy was the master of manipulation, but this was outright insanity!

Sara could not believe what she was hearing and that her mama actually believed him. Even in her youth and naiveté, Sara had the wisdom to know there was *no way* he could be a different person after only one visit to a psychiatrist. He had chosen a lifetime of vile behaviors and attitudes! Only

God could perform that kind of miracle, and it wasn't God to whom her daddy had gone.

Sara's mama was not at all confident in her ability to be alone or raise her three sons alone, and she didn't believe in divorce. She believed that divorce was wrong according to scriptures, and the church preached against it. Tragically, they didn't ever preach against the sin and destruction of abuse that had directly stemmed from their religious legalism, nor how unacceptable and dishonoring abuse is to God and how it destroys lives and families.

She wanted to believe her husband because she was too afraid to live life apart from him. He was all she had known and depended on for nearly twenty years and, oddly enough, still loved him.

Sara could tell by her mama's persuasive tone that she wanted Sara to believe him, too. Sara thought her mama had completely lost all logic. She tried frantically to reason with her that he was still the same person and could not have possibly changed. But still, her mama wanted to believe he had, and wanted Sara to believe it as well. She didn't—she couldn't.

"There are so many eyes on him now, holding him accountable," she countered. "He went before the church and apologized."

Good for him! Sara silently screamed to her mama sarcastically in her head. *But he didn't apologize to me!! I'm the one he sexually violated and beat all these years!* It sickened Sara to hear how gullible her mama was, and so desperately dependent on him. She couldn't believe how blind her mama was to him and couldn't believe she had allowed him to move back home and back into her family's life. *How could she?! Was she mad?*

It sickened Sara further when many years later she learned that he had not included in his public apology to their church exactly *how* he had sinned or that he had sinned against his own daughter. He had not stated to the congregation that he had forced his daughter into sexual relations with him night after night. The only thing the church members knew was that he had *somehow* sinned. The sin itself was left to whispered speculation among the people. The simple fact that he had gotten up publicly before them and confessed to a vague sin had apparently been all that was required of him to regain righteous standing in the eyes of the church.

Aunt Aggie and Uncle P. were equally stunned that Sara's mama had allowed him to move back home, and believed him to be a changed man—but not as shell-shocked as they all would soon be with the next phone call. None of them were prepared for the bomb that would hit them several days later when her mama called again.

Gingerly, with quiet hesitation, her mama said, "Sara, your daddy believes you should come back home…where you belong."

An electric-like shock riveted through Sara's head and raced through her body at this insane proclamation. Too stunned to speak and frozen with terror and shock, she nearly passed out on her aunt's cold kitchen floor.

"Sara?"

"No way!" She recovered and screamed. "I'm not going home! I'm not going back into that house with that monster!" She began to sob, fear and defeat wrapping around her like a python threatening to squeeze the life from her. All of the fears she had finally begun to put to rest since escaping him, suddenly rushed to the surface like a tidal wave drowning her. She was panicked and nauseated with fear. Hell had come back to claim her and devour her after all.

"It'll be okay, Sara. You'll see. He's really changed and wants the family to be back together … and you're still underage."

In his eyes, Sara was his property, and still legally under his jurisdiction. Having authority over Sara's mama for so many years, he was not easily dismissed. Sara wasn't even certain her mama had tried to persuade him against bringing her home. It sickened her.

As she listened in abhorrence, her world crumbled around her once again and the familiar fear that had plagued her for sixteen years rose up to strangle her. Again, she defiantly told her mama that she was not going back home to live in that house with him, under any circumstances. But the adamancy she expressed was not remotely confident within her. She was terrified that he would force her back home. He was far too manipulative and determined to allow his underage daughter to make any decisions against his desires and authority. She knew him well—and her mama well. It had been an isolated incident of uncharacteristic protection when her mama had temporarily intervened and taken her away to safety. It was completely unthinkable to Sara, but true to her mama's character that she would agree to bring Sara back home to her daddy's easy grasp.

Sara wept as she continued to plead with her mama to dissuade him from pursuing this. It was to no avail. Her mama continued to assure her that everything would be all right, and that it would be safe for Sara to return home. Sara knew better, and refused.

How can she possibly believe that everything will be all right? How can sixteen years of physical, sexual, mental, emotional, and spiritual abuse and trauma simply be swept under the rug—just like that!? Sara simply could not make sense of her mama's gross lack of judgment. She couldn't imagine going back to live in that house where so many horrors had taken place since her birth, and she couldn't imagine moving back in with that evil man.

That weekend, still terribly upset over her mama's phone call, and gripped with fear that they would force her to come back home, she decided it might do her good to spend the afternoon outdoors at the nearby reservoir where Uncle P. and his adult son—Sara's cousin—were planning to go fishing. Sara loved the outdoors. Creation had always brought her a sense of comfort and peace in the most horrid of times. The thought of sunshine warming her face and arms, and the lake breeze blowing her hair, prompted her to go with them instead of shopping with her aunt.

Once they arrived at the lake, she decided to stay near the small clearing at the edge of the lake where they'd parked. Her uncle and cousin disappeared through the patch of woods lining the lake shore to fish some distance away, leaving her alone.

The feel of the sunshine, the glimmer of the vast lake, the beauty of tiny, autumn wild flowers forming a colorful brigade, the sounds of insects—living free, without fear— all nurtured Sara's heart, mind, and emotions like a healing balm. Immersing herself in the beauty and solitude of nature had helped her survive the dark and seemingly endless years of her childhood.

As habit, Sara peered down the highway whenever she

heard a vehicle approaching from the distance. Few cars passed along that stretch of highway, so with each one, a little anxiety arose in her. She was afraid of people and thus afraid of being discovered alone by some passing stranger. The thought of strangers catching sight of her, alone, heightened Sara's awareness to the sights and sounds around her. She still lived in a constant state of apprehension of others, even her peers, though it had subsided somewhat when she had settled into a new life away from her daddy. Fear had always been part of the core fabric of her life. It was how she had been conditioned to live. She had just survived the worst living nightmare at the hands of her own daddy, and now they were threatening to bring her back into that nightmare. He and her mama were the two people in whom she was *supposed* to have had the greatest trust and security. If she couldn't trust her own parents to protect her, how could she possibly trust a stranger passing along the highway? She couldn't. She could trust no one.

Sara was trying to relax and enjoy the beauty and warmth of the day when she heard another vehicle approaching from the distance. She glanced up … but what she saw barreling toward her this time paralyzed her. Another real nightmare was unfolding before her eyes—her daddy and mama had found her.

She learned later that they had first stopped at her aunt and uncle's house and found no one home, so they traveled about the small town in search of Sara. As fate would have it, they had come upon her by the lake.

Frozen in place, she screamed and screamed for her uncle and cousin as she watched her daddy and mama's car pull in and stop only five feet from her. But her uncle and cousin never came. She would later learn that they had never heard her screams. She had been so disabled by fear that no sound had come out of her mouth, although she was screaming with everything in her. In shock and acting like a panicked, wild animal, she skirted around the vehicles, shaking her head no, and crying. She could hardly talk, she was so debilitated and stunned over their sudden appearance—out of nowhere! She had been anxious of strangers passing by, but the reality was that she was most fearful of her own daddy. How tragic.

Her mama quietly and gently tried to assure Sara and convince her that everything would be okay. Sara saw on her mama's face and in her eyes the resignation to the control her husband had over her, as he had for so many years. It was a very familiar look on her mama's face. Nothing had changed—*nothing*! Sara couldn't believe her mama had gotten sucked back under his control after all they had been through. She couldn't believe that her mama had agreed to bring her back home, knowing full well how he had violated Sara and mistreated her physically for years. It was insane!

She saw the familiar impatience growing on her daddy's face. Nothing had changed in him; he was still as powerful and manipulative as he had always been. He held all the cards because there was no one, except perhaps her aunt and uncle, who would stand up for her and see how insane all of this was, but they were not coming to her rescue; they didn't know she was in trouble. *Where are they?* She frantically looked around.

Getting in the car with him and going back to live with him in that house of horrors was an emotional death sentence for Sara. She knew this and was panicked that they might physically force her into the car. Would she ever escape him for good? Would Aunt Aggie and Uncle P. come to her rescue? Would they stand up for her against him?

As she feared, he forced her into the car, and her mama allowed it. Nothing had changed. Sara had no choice that she could recognize through conditioned fear. She was still a child held hostage by the years of abusive authority that demanded she obey—or else. She knew no power. She was going back home.

Chapter Twelve

Aunt Aggie and Uncle P. had no clue that Sara's parents had arrived in town unannounced, nor that they had stopped by the house to get Sara. They had no idea that Sara's mama and daddy had found her by the lake and forced her into the car.

Sara's mama was grateful to her sister and brother-in-law for taking Sara in and caring for her. So they wouldn't worry, she at least wanted to stop by their house before they took Sara home with them, to tell them they were taking her and to retrieve her few belongings. But Sara's daddy wouldn't consider it. He intended to drive the two hours straight home from the lake where he had, in essence, kidnapped Sara.

Years later, looking back, Sara believed her daddy had to have been too ashamed to face his wife's family. He knew they had been told the atrocities he had committed against his daughter. But Sara was not so convinced that *he* viewed his actions as atrocities, but rather as his *right*. His skewed thinking was very hard for her to comprehend. She was trying to make some kind of sense out of all those years of abuse and obsession, but no matter how she looked at it, it was insane and abhorrent. There was no justifiable explanation for abuse of any kind or any degree. He had to have been mentally ill and/or dominated or possessed by evil. There were no other explanations.

Her mama tried to reason with him as to why they should stop by Aggie's house before heading back home. "Perin will be worried *sick* at finding Sara missing from the lake, and so will Aggie when they come home and tell her she's disappeared! We just can't do that to them." But Sara's daddy didn't care about anything or anyone except himself and his own agenda, as usual. In that moment, Sara knew for certain that he had not changed. She couldn't reconcile in her mind how her mama had fallen back under his control, after all she had seen and all she knew to be true.

Her daddy was totally without regard to the panic and chaos his actions were generating in Sara. He was without regard that her aunt and uncle would be frantic over her disappearance. He was without regard to his wife's desire to stop and put her sister and brother-in-law at ease. He was without regard to the value Sara placed in her few belongings left at her aunt's house. He was simply without regard to anyone but himself.

Oh, God… oh, God… Sara cried out and pled in her heart as her tiny body shook with fear, gulping in air, tears streaming down her face. *Please, please don't let them take me back home with them ... please.*

Sara's mama continued to persuade him to see reason and finally convinced him to drive to her sister's house, "So we can at least gather Sara's things and put their minds at ease."

His relenting gave Sara a glint of hope that her aunt and uncle would try to convince her daddy to allow her to stay and finish her senior year of high school. Surely, her aunt and uncle would come to her defense and not allow him to take her back home. She prayed and prayed as she sobbed, her body shaking uncontrollably at the thought of journeying back to hell. Everything she had gained over the past three months was whisked away. She was again robbed and devastated by the devil himself.

She knew her daddy so well. She knew her chances of ever escaping him again were slim. She was physically ill at this new, living nightmare she'd been forced to re-enter. In her heart she cried out again and again, *why, oh why did she bring me back into this situation? How can she possibly believe he has changed?*

Nothing made sense to Sara—nothing! It was all wrong. It was all hopeless! It was mad! Sara's whole life had been one long, perpetual nightmare, only sprinkled sparingly here and there with a little reprieve, a little joy and sunshine from time to time, short-lived.

True to Sara's hope, Aunt Aggie and Uncle P. came to her defense. Not long after Sara had been kidnapped from the lake, Uncle P. and Sara's cousin had discovered her missing and anxiously searched for her, then headed home to see if she had been picked up by Aggie on her way home from shopping. They arrived home just shortly after Sara and her parents arrived.

They did not want to see Sara go back home with her daddy. It was tragic to even consider. They did their best, short of physically hanging on to Sara, to convince him to allow her to stay. As they haggled over her fate, Sara was so distraught and emotionally out of control that she sat down on the floor in a corner, in desperation and defeat, and sobbed and retched. It didn't matter the havoc he was inflicting in her life, or what was truly best for her. Only his own desires mattered—as they always had.

In the end, Aggie and Perin were unable to persuade him to allow her to stay. She was going back home. The road back to hell was a long one.

Chapter Thirteen

Sara re-entered her old high school, numb and lifeless. She cared about nothing anymore except dying. The only glimmer of hope she still had was to convince her daddy to let her go to college where Allie was attending. A six-hour drive would put a good distance between her and her daddy.

Since Allie had been allowed to move out to attend the one school he approved of, it gave Sara hope that she could escape him by following in her sister's footsteps. She told her parents that she wanted to attend the seminary as well, after she graduated the following spring. However, her daddy announced that she wasn't going anywhere until she paid back every penny that her aunt and uncle had spent on her private schooling, clothing, and expenses. He was going to try every means and excuse possible to keep her there with him for as long as he could. Again, Sara lost hope that she would ever be able to escape him.

The expenses of her private schooling, generously paid by her aunt and uncle without expectation or desire for repayment, were exorbitant in Sara's view. Aunt Aggie and Uncle P. didn't want Sara to repay them, and they told her daddy so, but he was the authority over Sara—not them. Sara knew it wasn't at all about the money. It was about his own pious pride, power, and desire to keep her home with him. Her only hope was to work hard and fast to repay the expenses, so she dedicated herself to that end.

Through the school's work-study program again, Sara was able to work throughout the remainder of her senior year to earn money, only attending classes in the mornings. She taught piano in the evenings and also took a job at the local mall on Saturdays. She sent money regularly to her aunt and uncle. She also purchased her own used car and clothing so she had no further obligation that he might hold over her at a later date.

During that year and a half back at home, Sara continued to fight horrific nightmares, panic attacks, and a host of physical and emotional difficulties consequential to post-traumatic and on-going stress at returning to her daddy's authority and that hell house again.

Strange things began to manifest in her physically from the stress and trauma. She had never been able to stop biting her nails, still jerked her head and arm whenever she was overwrought, and constantly worked at hiding these embarrassments from others. She persistently bit her lips and tore up the insides of her cheeks. But stranger things developed as well. She began to lose the feeling in her upper right leg and hip, intermittently. She'd sometimes have difficulty walking. It felt as though a part of her leg had suddenly been amputated. She didn't know what was happening to her, which fed her anxiety more.

She continued to have moments when she simply could not breathe. It was as though the involuntary function of her lungs suddenly ceased and she'd have to consciously, manually, inhale and exhale.

Her clothes never felt comfortable on her because her skin felt extraordinarily sensitive. She could feel every hair, every particle, like her nerve endings were on high alert. This hypersensitivity was another constant irritant, along with her perpetually aching and raw fingernails, mouth, and head.

She'd have terrible headaches from jerking her head and from sheer stress, and began taking a host of pain killers that would cause other adverse side affects—either speeding or falling asleep. Simply put, at seventeen, she was a mess—mentally, emotionally, and physically. Her parent's never seemed to notice—or just simply didn't care. She knew her daddy didn't care—that was a given—but she believed her mama did and just didn't have the backbone to stand up and care for her children as she should have. Aside from true freedom from her daddy, there was nothing Sara wanted more than death.

♥ ♥ ♥

An important survival tool for Sara during her senior year back home was creative writing, which was encouraged and nurtured in her Senior English class. She wrote many simplistic poems that mirrored her hope, faith, and the deep pain of her life. Her poetry entwined nature with emotion that simply brought her peace and fueled her to keep moving toward her goal—freedom.

Sunshine smile and take my hand–
   lead me on
      where I might stand ... push the darkness out of sight
             wrap my heart
                  within your light.
Show me things I might not see–
   lift me up
      and laugh with me ... even through showers
        you make things right–
           thank you for the rainbow sight.

♥ ♥ ♥

Mirror of truth
   examiner to be–

         not of you ...
         only of me.
Mirror of truth
   reflection I see–

         fear within ...
         reality.
Mirror of truth
   clearly has shown–

         hopelessly helpless,
          the way that I roam.
Mirror of truth
   examiner to be–

         not of you ...
         only of me.

♥ ♥ ♥

Have you ever touched a rainbow?
Have you ever kissed a star?
Have you ever wished that happiness
Didn't seem quite so far?
Have you ever planted daisies,
Watched them wake up with the sun?
Have you ever wished that morning
Would just hurry up and come?
Have you ever floated on a cloud
Or whispered to the moon?
Have you ever feared that 'special one'
Would leave you much too soon?
If I could live forever
I'd gather stardust for my food
I'd ride upon an ocean wave
And dress in sunset's hue.
If I could live forever
I could take away the pain
And let my heart be filled with love
Myself to solely gain.

♥ ♥ ♥

She was rarely allowed to date. As a matter of fact, she was only allowed to date one young man from church, whose parents were greatly respected by her daddy. The few times she was allowed to go to dinner with him, there were very strict rules her daddy imposed and always an interrogation when she returned home. It was hardly worth the effort to date.

It was senseless to even ask if she could date a boy from

school. She knew for a fact that her daddy would never allow it. Resentful toward him, she knew she had to reject every offer that came her way. It was the same with extra curricular school activities, like football games, invitations to parties, and other normal high school activities. She practiced piano instead—another outlet; another means of escape.

She was an advanced pianist by her senior year, practicing as much as four hours straight every night. Playing the piano, getting lost in that ethereal world of touch and sound, and the power that playing evoked in her, was an important outlet. She could lose herself in the beautiful sounds she strived to achieve and loved the feel of the cool keys on her fingertips.

Because her daddy always left her alone whenever she was practicing and mandated that the family leave her alone as well, she often stayed on the bench late into the evenings, playing until she literally fell asleep at the keyboard. Like nodding off late at night in bed while trying to read a good book, Sara would nod off at the piano as she played.

Night after night, she threw all her anger and resentments, all her hopes and dreams, into the keys. She would get caught up in the powerful feeling produced by hammering the keys and hearing the amazing sounds in response, driving her to extend her whole heart and soul through her fingertips. But it was never enough to satisfy the fury or the longing within her. Being in command of the piano and the piece she was playing, determining how the keys would respond was powerful. She was in control of something. She had power over something. She had nothing else in her life that she had ever been allowed to command or control. Her daddy had stripped every attempt of control and power from her through his belt and through his manipulations and intimidations for seventeen relentless years.

Too often, though, she felt the piano still mastered her, no matter how many lessons she took and no matter how long or how often she practiced. The complete satisfaction was always just out of reach, no matter how hard she tried to grasp it. Not unlike trying to escape her daddy—reaching and striving for freedom but never quite getting there. Regardless, she didn't give up on either. She loved to play the piano and loved the challenge. She would not only be consumed by the sensory effects but also by the opaque, emotional escape it afforded.

Piano, writing, reading, and church were her only extra curricular activities. There were no sports, no clubs...certainly no parties or dances, and no senior prom. It made the large and very active youth group at church all the more appealing. Those were her closest friends, many of whom she had been born and raised with. Those were the friends who meant everything to her, but not at the cost of remaining at home. *Nothing* was worth staying home. Getting out of that house and never returning was worth the loss of all else in her life—even the loss of her own life.

Chapter Fourteen

Sara never tried to reach David after her parents forced her to return home. Her three months out of state in a refreshing and freeing new atmosphere, beginning her senior year in a new school with new friends, having the freedom to date all helped her to reconcile and somewhat heal from the loss of her first, true love. She still held a soft and generous place in her heart for him, but knew it would never work out for them to be together. Her only goal now was to get as far away as she could from her daddy, which meant following her sister to school—six hours away from home. That represented freedom to her.

When she graduated high school in the late spring of 1978, she secured full-time work in the state capitol. She was able to work forty hours a week with fairly decent pay, given her previous work history and recommendations. In addition, she continued to earn money in the evenings, teaching piano to young beginners. She traveled from home to home in the old, pale blue Vega she had purchased with her summer earnings. She needed every penny she could get to pay off the debts her daddy had mandated so she could finally move out by the only acceptable escape route—attending seminary with Allie. She longed for that day and could hardly even imagine what it would be like to be gone from him for good, and live in the freedom she had only hoped for.

Conflicting emotions regarding Allie's freedom stirred within her. On the one hand, she envied the freedom her sister was enjoying, out from under their daddy's authority. On the other hand, she was happy that Allie no longer had to live within his immutable grasp. *Will my time ever come?* She still had only a faint light at the end of the terrifying, dark corridor she journeyed toward freedom. She couldn't even count the days until she could leave because she didn't know how long it would take to satisfy her debts. Seeing on paper the amount she owed her aunt and uncle felt overwhelming and unattainable. It was certainly worth the effort, though, if he would truly let her leave once the debts were paid.

She knew there was no way, on her meager earnings, that she could fulfill the financial burden by fall, only three months away when she could have otherwise left for school. Realistically, she was looking at another full year before she would see a zero balance, hopefully by the time school would resume the following fall. Her escape seemed forever out of reach, ever dim, ever prolonged, ever hopeless, but she refused to give up. Without *hope and faith* there truly was nothing left. Her life, her sanity, her future, depended on the hope of certain escape, and the faith that she would reach the exit door to freedom.

It was exciting to have landed a job in the state capitol. The qualities she offered would appeal to any employer. She was a very hard worker, a perfectionist, and fearfully respectful of her superiors, qualities branded in her psyche by the searing iron of discipline and punishment under her daddy's merciless expectations. He'd taught her to be highly self-conscious, deeply insecure, and unquenchably needy. He'd taught her to be fearful of all who were in authority—school, church, work, society—especially men. Thus, she was quick to please her employers, always placing other's desires and needs above her own and to exceed excellence in everything she did. She was set up for constant failure because perfection was impossible. Consequently, if anyone—an employer, teacher, friend— showed the slightest dissatisfaction, weariness, or irritation, toward her for whatever reason, she would quickly plunge into dark despair. She never, ever felt good enough, skilled enough, loved enough, or even liked enough. She would fall so hard over the slightest dissatisfactions or altercations that she'd lose sleep with worry, she'd vomit, have diarrhea, weep, and even entertain suicidal thoughts over truly insignificant things. She'd feel utterly worthless and unworthy.

Working in the state capitol exposed her to a variety of people and experiences, as the newspaper had. Once again, the attention Sara began to get from men in the work place made her feel wanted and valued, still her greatest emotional needs.

Sully was fifteen years older than Sara and divorced with two preteen children. She couldn't believe the attention he was giving her because inside she felt so inadequate and worthless. His attention made her feel really good—like a highly addictive drug. The more attention she got, the more she desperately craved it, not realizing she had a core need that had been deprived since her birth.

> God intended for daddies to be to their daughters a direct reflection of God Himself: his pure and unconditional love, gentleness, kindness, compassion, encouragement, justice, and other Godly characteristics that form a solid foundation of security and value that enables a little girl to grow up *whole*.
>
> *Little girls need their daddy's love.* Girls who do not get from their daddies the love, security, and value that God entrusted their daddies to give, will seek out all of these things when they are young women, in any place and in any form they can get it.
>
> This is a proven fact through the ages. We all have an inherent need to be loved and cherished, to receive protection, security, and correct training according to God's characteristics and principles. God intended for little girls to receive these things from their daddies.

Sully wooed Sara, and she believed everything he said. He took her to lunches and quickly began to gain her trust, just as David had. After all, he was a nice man. He was kind. She could trust him. She could not have been more thrilled and excited that a man of his maturity and position would even give her a second glance. She didn't really understand how or why she was attracting older men, but it nurtured and fed her starving self-esteem.

By the time he persuaded her into his bed, she truly believed he cared for her. Why would he otherwise pay her so much attention, be so nice, and take her to lunch through the work week? Ignorant to men and the ways of human nature and the world, she was under his spell. Her emotional needs ran deep and heavy, like an undernourished, ravenous, mistreated animal. His attention was addictive, like David's had been. She just couldn't get enough and wanted to replace what she had lost with David. She clung to Sully. She took every possible opportunity she could manage to see him outside of work. This was difficult because of the stringent confines and control she was under, living at home.

Her only real freedom outside the forty hours she worked during the week was the scheduled evenings she traveled to teach piano to young students in their homes. She also took every opportunity on Saturdays to volunteer to run errands for her daddy or mama so she could sneak opportunity to call and go visit Sully. They were glad she could drive and save them the trips to the hardware store, lumberyard, auto supply store, or grocery. Any chance she had to get out of the house alone, she took eagerly, and with calculation. She'd stop at pay phones hoping to catch Sully at home, and make quick trips to see him whenever possible. On one such trip, she met his two preteen daughters. It struck her how there were so few years between her age and theirs. Still, she fantasized about a life with them as step-mom, and wife to Sully. She was so naive to the dynamics and challenges of adult relationships. She believed that happiness existed everywhere but in her own home, and she was anxious for the happiness the rest of the world seemed to share.

Sara had no clue of the realities of being a wife, other than what she observed in her own mama—and she was determined to never live like her mama had. And she certainly had no understanding of the natural and manufactured difficulties of being a step-mom—especially to teenage girls barely younger than herself. From her narrow worldview, naiveté, and skewed perspective she became certain of a few things she believed to be true: One. Men were attentive and kind to her simply because they were nice men, except for her own daddy. Other daddies were loving and caring toward their children; therefore, her daddy must be among only a few who were not. Two. She would never live as her own mama did, under the control and authority of a man, much less an abusive one. Three. Other marriages were not like her parent's. Every adult couple she had ever known and observed through the years appeared to be happy. Four. She loved children and would be a good and loving mom, whether to step-children or children of her own.

In reality, blinded by innocence, the last was the only truth among the four. It would take her a long time to reconcile the other three.

Another reality she didn't recognize was that Sully had no interest in her other than to enjoy her young body. She was easy to play. When Sully grew tired of her and abruptly ended their relationship, it was another crushing blow to her and again reinforced her feelings of worthlessness. She didn't understand what she had done to make him dislike her now. *Have I done something to upset him?* She searched their stolen times together. *I've tried to please him and bring him happiness,* she mourned. He had been so attentive and caring… *What's wrong with me that no one loves me?* She cried, not understanding. Her own daddy didn't love her, but he didn't pretend to either. On the other hand, David and Sully had both shown her again and again how much they liked her… then abandoned her. *There must be something wrong with me,* she disparaged.

She simply didn't understand and was deeply depressed and heartbroken over this third loss of love. Her emotional need, coupled with her losses, made her all too ripe for the next man who pursued her on the heels of Sully's departure. She would try harder this time.

Ted was also older, by ten years, and divorced with a baby. He was well educated, very funny, and he paid a whole lot of attention to Sara. He also worked in the same department in the capitol with her and Sully, though he and Sully were never friends. Ted constantly teased and flirted with her, drawing her in. She could tell that he liked her, but she didn't know why. She was always a little taken back when a man showed her attention, but she liked it—a lot.

She'd have to be careful how she interacted with Ted, so he wouldn't find something wrong with her, as the other men in her life had. As she had all her life with her daddy, she was careful to measure her words with Ted, tried extra hard to please and to be perfect so he wouldn't stop liking her and toss her aside as well. She worked hard to always look nice, always appear happy, not complain about anything, or reveal too much of her true self because her true self must be flawed. She worked extra hard at giving, caring, and being attentive, so he would not grow tired of being with her. With each relationship she was moving farther and farther from the truth, and digging a deeper grave for herself.

It was easier for her to be persuaded into Ted's bed because life experiences were teaching her that in order to be loved and valued she would have to give her body in exchange. After all, she was beginning to feel that it was only her body, her looks, that made her worthwhile or worthy of love.

Men were drawn to her like bees to nectar, and she began to learn to use their desires to try and fulfill her own—her insatiable need to be found worthy, valued, and loved. She needed to feel these things in order to have any reason at all to hope and live. She couldn't get enough of the attention that men cast her way. It was as though they were throwing small cubes of stew meat to a ravenous lion. It was just never, ever enough to fill her and created in her a further hunger. Her emotional well was not only dry, it was bottomless. She didn't realize any of this—at all.

She was tiny and petite, worked very hard at being attractive every time she stepped out of the house, very careful to act happy and be sweet, eager to please. She was naive, pure, and virginal by nature … easy prey. She was more than willing to work hard to be everything a man would want because she was so desperately hungry for acceptance. She didn't understand, or even have a clue, that the kind of love they easily offered was short lived and held a condition—not the kind of love that would truly satisfy her emotionally. It would be a long, difficult journey to reach this realization.

Chapter Fifteen

Her year of working to pay back her debts was drawing to an end. Far greater than her need for Ted's love was her desperate need to escape her daddy. As much as she loved Ted (though an unhealthy, desperate, and needy love), she hated and feared her daddy more, far outweighing all else in life. She had to either escape him somehow or die. There were no other choices in Sara's mind.

She lived in perpetual pretense. Life was her stage and she was the consummate actress in order to survive. No one knew the depth of her pain, resentment, fear, and needs. She learned from a very young age how to pretend that everything was okay in order to avoid further upset and punishment. The term "walking on eggshells" was the epitome of her daily life. What alternative did she have if she wanted to avoid retaliation and survive? Had she shown her true colors to her daddy—the way she really felt about him—perhaps there would have been no waiting. Perhaps he would have simply thrown her out! She hadn't known any other way through life than fear and pretense. It was what it was. She was well conditioned to bow to his authority—and the authority of other adults.

He had relentlessly held her tightly in his fist, choking all the life out of her; but now he had no more reasons or excuses to hold her at home. She had legally been an adult for a year, now nineteen, and had paid her debts—or so her daddy thought. As she approached her nineteenth birthday, Aunt Aggie knew full well how desperately she needed to flee from him, and that school was her only sensible recourse, so she privately told Sara that as far as she and Uncle P. were concerned, her debts were fully paid. She should send no more money.

The slate had been wiped clean by her aunt and uncle. They had again rescued and sheltered her. They had not wanted her to repay them in the first place, but they knew the best strategy for her peace and safety was to allow her to show her daddy that she was obeying him by sending money to them each week. He didn't keep track of the records, though; only Sara and her aunt kept track of her payments and balance. In reality, the debts were really *his*. He was the abuser who had forced his own daughter from home with a nervous breakdown at sixteen, and had put into motion the events that incurred those expenses. Yet, she had to pay. She had always had to pay for *his* sins. She had been paying for his sins her entire life in one form or another. Now he had nothing further he might use to hold over her. He could no longer keep her at home. Freedom—*real freedom*—was finally, blessedly at the door for Sara, and she was determined to walk through that door, still pretending that everything was okay.

♥ ♥ ♥

The day that Sara's mama and daddy left her at school in another state, six hours away, was *the* happiest day of Sara's life to that point. For the first time in her life, she experienced true freedom. The choices that freedom brought were staggering. She had been held in such tight reign for so many years. Now, suddenly, she could go anywhere she wanted; she could do anything she pleased. It was an *amazing* feeling, one she embraced with fervor.

To shop for groceries, go to her first movie, get her ears pierced, date whomever she pleased, make new friends, come and go at will—apart from her daddy's authority and ever-watchful eyes—was what she had longed for, prayed for, and wept over for so long. Everything that life offered now, no matter how mundane to others, was new and exciting and freeing for Sara. Life was now 'live-giving.'

With her newfound freedom, Sara pushed the previous nineteen years of hell as far back into the recesses of her mind as possible. She never again wanted to think about her former life, but fully embrace this new one. She would never go back—never. She had her own life now, so full of possibilities and unfettered options. She was free at last! She never again wanted to see her daddy or think about all the years of horror, suffering, and despair. At last, her prayers had been answered—she was free!

♥ ♥ ♥

Sara lived in an apartment on campus with three roommates. One afternoon, she arrived home to an empty apartment and retrieved the mail. To her surprise and quick annoyance, there was a cassette tape from her daddy. She knew right away it was from him. There was no mistaking his *fancy* penmanship. Just seeing her name scrawled across the thick, white envelope by his unique hand immediately caused her heart to plummet to her stomach. The same hand that had abused her so cruelly, the hand that had beaten, stripped, raped, and robbed her to the very core.

To her further dismay and horror, she uncovered a love note in his distinctive handwriting, scripted on a photograph of a rose. The too familiar bile of hatred rose to her throat. Seeing his handwriting and reading the nauseous note was like a punch in her stomach; but it was the cassette tape that did her in. Not knowing what was on the tape, her mind whirled in a million directions as she slipped it into the stereo system. Suddenly shattering the afternoon quietness were the love songs he used to sing to her as a teen, when he'd make her scoot over next to him in the car, as if she was his girlfriend. He had never changed. He was still obsessed with her.

Every horror of her past that she had buried suddenly charged to the forefront like the explosion of a gun. Consumed and drowning in the swirling sewer of her past, she ran from her apartment, crying … she didn't know where to run, but this time had the freedom. She didn't know who to run to, but this time there were people who would care.

She remembers reaching the covered walk just outside her

apartment door … and this is where her memory ends. Years later, Sara would recognize that she had dissociated again, losing a period of time from her memory. Her mind could not handle the sudden flooding in of all those thoughts of abuse, his sickening touch and obsessive words while also trying to register her present surroundings. The flashback to her past had fully captured her mind and became her reality.[6]

The next thing Sara remembered was waking up in the night darkness of Allie's bedroom where she and her husband lived across town. *How did I get here?* She squinted in the dim light, her mind a fog. The last thing she recalled was running out of her apartment, crying, and why. The stench bile of remembrance lay thick on her mind and her stomach. Hot tears of frustration, resentment, fear, and hatred burned her eyes. Even in her freedom, she was still bound by him and still pursued by him.

Sara got up in search of Allie and was greeted not only by her sister and brother-in-law, but also by the Dean of Women and her husband from school. They informed Sara that her sister had bravely called their daddy and told him to never again make any contact with Sara. With his obsession of Sara and instability of mind, no one in the small group knew how he might respond. Would he immediately hop in his car and travel the six hours to reclaim ownership? What? Sara was visibly shaken, terrified that he would, in fact, show up. Again, she asked herself if she would ever escape him. She sobbed as she pondered what his recourse might be, and how to protect herself.

It was very possible that he would show up at her apartment, so she knew she could not return there. Neither could she stay at Allie's apartment for the same reason. He could easily locate her on campus or at Allie's apartment. Would he come after her that very night? The next day? She needed to be in the protection of an adult who would stand up for her in the event that he came to town and made a scene.

The Dean of Women and her husband insisted she go home with them. They would shelter and protect her through this crisis. Her daddy didn't know them, or where they lived. Their home would be her safe house until they were all satisfied he would leave her alone. She and Allie agreed that she should go home with her Dean. This was the second time in her young life that she had been spirited away in protection from her daddy. Would it never end?

Over the next week, she didn't attend classes. She stayed hidden away in fear from what might be, should her daddy materialize. She had not reached a point of maturity or strength to stand up against him alone. She needed protection.

A week went by without a word from him. It became apparent that he was not going to show up after all, so Sara cautiously returned to her apartment and friends, and resumed her classes and freedom, though she constantly looked over her shoulder. Although he never tried to contact her again, it would be many years before she would be freed from the emotional rags he had tightly bound her in like a mummy, paralyzed and suffocating.

Chapter Sixteen

Sara needed a man in order to feel loved and to feed her insatiable, emotional hunger that gnawed at her every waking hour. Her voracious need for acceptance, affection, and attention took precedence over everything else in her life—school, church, work, girlfriends ... God. She was simply *lost* and emotionally paralyzed apart from a male. Without continual affirmations, she fell desperate, became incapacitated, and simply felt no reason to live.

She didn't know how to begin to love herself or how to recognize and embrace all the good qualities that made her as unique, special, and valuable as the next person. She didn't know how to exist apart from a man. Consequently, every man she was attracted to, who showed interest in pursuing a relationship with her, she clung to, soaking up every drop of attention

JEN MILLER

and affection he would give. It was easy for her to fall hard and fast for a man she was attracted to and in turn was attracted to her. Naturally, she got hurt easily and often because no one could give her what she needed emotionally. Nonetheless, she experienced a great deal of fun in her newfound freedom, dating a variety of young men, but only feeling affirmed as a human being when she was vested in a relationship.

While she dated a lot and gained many friendships, she also maintained a long-distance relationship with Ted by phone. Despite all the guys her own age that she was dating and the geographical distance between her and Ted, he still held Sara's intrigue and gained more and more of her heart. Their lengthy, long-distance phone conversations fed and fueled Sara's heart toward him. He invested himself in her a lot through their conversations night after night. He drew her in, just as he had when they had worked together the year prior.

He was much older than all the young men she dated from school and work. Older men were far more appealing to Sara than her peers. She didn't know why, or really even consider the possible reasons. She didn't recognize the truth that she was always on the hunt for the father figure she had never had and instinctively needed. This hidden fact aside, she intuitively surmised correctly that she was attracted to older men because she had been through so much in life that it was difficult to relate to the silliness, antics, and immaturity of younger men, her peers. Both were true, but only one she recognized at that time. Some young men were more mature than others, but they all seemed too young to her, except one—Nick.

Nick was Sara's age and very mature, together, and

grounded. He was highly attractive and kind, and shared a lot in common with Sara. He was a gifted musician—a keyboardist and vocalist like herself. Sara found him to be humble and very encouraging of her own talents. She was very shy around him when it came to music because she had no confidence in herself whatsoever. She refused to play or sing for him, even though music was her focus of education at school, and she had to perform regularly. She was so in awe of his abilities and so insecure in her own that she was too intimidated to play or sing for him.

He fell quickly for Sara, as she did for him. They had a lot of fun and spent as much time together as possible around school, music performances, and work responsibilities. As their relationship grew, he introduced her to his family—a wealthy, catholic family.

Although Nick cared a great deal for Sara, in the end he broke her heart, too, just like David, Sully, and her dad had, but for very different reasons. She was not from an affluent family and far, far from catholic. His parents found her completely unacceptable for Nick and demanded that he end their relationship in favor of a "more suitable match." Sara was devastated again. She was utterly heartbroken and could hardly function for weeks and had no desire to. Allie, along with Sara's roommates, nursed her through the roughest days and helped her to see reality and logic. None of it changed the way she felt inside though.

What's wrong with me that I'm so unacceptable? Where am I acceptable? She had never been acceptable to her daddy, until she had developed into a young woman. She had been abandoned by her mama, David, Sully, and now Nick. And by the school's legalistic standards, she was too much a "rebellious believer," as she coined it, so she was not acceptable there, either.

She would not subscribe to the legalism they demanded their students live by. Their religious statutes were more of the same she had been raised under, an extension of her home church, which she naturally rebelled against. Unknown to the powers-that-be at the school, the only reason she was there in the first place was to free herself from her daddy's divisive clutches. That particular school had offered her the only legitimate escape route to ease out from under his paralyzing authority. Although she had achieved a greater level of freedom than she had ever known, she was still under legalistic, religious authority as a student. While she blossomed in her newfound freedom, she suffocated under the oppressive limitations placed on her by the school in the name of God. The two positive aspects of school were the continued music education she gained, and freedom from her daddy.

The breakup with Nick caused her to cling further to her friendship with Ted, as much as she could with the geographical distance between them. She continued to date other young men, but in the end she grew more attached to Ted. She decided it was Ted who could truly bring her happiness. He never seemed to tire of her, or demand anything from her. And, he was the only one who had not left her—yet—so perhaps he did really care about her, she concluded.

To her skewed way of thinking, Ted represented everything she was missing and needing in life, though if you had asked her she would not have been able to put a finger on what it was exactly that she *truly* needed. She was clueless as to how tragically the wires of her psyche had been disordered—rewired—by ill-treatment. She had not been exposed to the truth that true happiness and fulfillment is not dependent upon another person. No one had taught her or shown her that true happiness and fulfillment could only be achieved from knowing and embracing her true self, as seen through the eyes of God, her Creator. She didn't have a clue how intimately God knew her and loved her—far more than any other person could ever know and love her. It would be a long time before she would gain these truths that would ultimately and truly make her free.

Through the eyes of her blinded heart, she saw Ted as her knight on the white horse, ready, willing, and able to whisk her away to her fairytale world of never-ending love, joy, and freedom. To complete her fairytale, she would get to play mommy to his adorable two-year-old son. The perfect family and perfect life she had always hoped for, and survived for.

As she had with David, she played through her head all the scenarios of a "happy home" convinced that Ted would afford her this wonderful life. And she loved the idea of being a mommy; she always had. She had a deep compassion and love for children that had grown out of her own childhood of horrors and fear and the contrasting joy of playing mommy to her youngest brother, Wayne. She was eight-years-old when he was born and immediately adopted him as her live baby doll. She carried him around, played with him, nurtured him, cared for him, protected him (against the natural sibling rivalry of her two other brothers), and showed him unconditional love.

She had a natural instinct toward mothering and could hardly wait to grow up and have a child of her own. Thoughts of other children surviving a life of terror and abuse, as she had, made her sick. As a teenager, working with young children in her church, she had taken every opportunity to show them love and affection with enthusiasm and energy. Few could incite smiles, laughter, and excited animation from children like Sara could. It came natural to her out of her own hunger. She longed for a child of her own to love and to love her.

She loved the idealism of setting up her own house and playing wife and mommy to a husband and child who loved her as deeply as she would love them. She was convinced she would have her heart's desires met through Ted, as simple as they were. She believed he would provide a ready-made life and family dramatically different from the one she had been raised in. She just hoped that he would always adore her, want her, and respect her as he appeared to in that moment.

He was well established in his career, represented himself to be mature and secure, loving and caring, funny and attentive … she desperately craved and valued these qualities. There was only one drawback to the fairytale—location. She would have to move back to her home state, to her home city, face all the familiar surroundings of her growing up years and—worst of all—risk running into her dad. It wasn't "Neverland" or "Oz;" however, Sara decided Ted's love and a life with him was worth the risk.

Sara had no desire to stay in the confines and oppression of the school she attended, especially when her greatest dreams were now within reach, with Ted. Her emotional needs were too overpowering to stop and consider the benefits of continuing her education and the opportunities it would afford her later in life. The only guidance she had had about furthering her education was that higher education would do her no good, according to daddy. There had been no college and career guidance at home. If there had been a teacher or counselor at school who had taken her under their wing to advise her, she didn't remember it. Much of her school memories were vague because her mind had been perpetually occupied with surviving. There had been no one to help Sara strategize her future toward becoming *all* she could be and desired to be—no one. At that moment, the only future she could imagine with liberated joy was a life with Ted. He would fulfill her emotional needs. So, she quit school and moved back to her home city.

At first, she acquired her own apartment and settled in to freely and openly date Ted. She had not had that freedom when she first met him. She had still been living at home and was highly restricted in her coming and going. She had been limited to seeing him only during the work day and the occasional opportunities they took during work hours to play hooky. They'd take short day trips on his motorcycle, picnics in the park, and other daytime activities whenever they could manage—always unbeknown to Sara's dad, who was confined to his own job from eight to five.

Sara was ecstatic over thoughts of having no more authority lording over her and the freedom to do whatever she pleased. Her dad was no longer a part of her life since the night Allie had called him in Sara's defense and protection. Now she could freely and openly spend time with Ted, doing whatever they wished, whenever they wished.

She relished and valued this new and greater level of freedom. Independence fueled in her enough joy and excitement to override some of her fear of her dad that lingered like a dark shadow in the peripherals of her mind, especially now that she was living and working in the same city where he worked.

While it was an exciting new adventure to have her own apartment, she was living alone for the very first time in her life, and still lived in constant fear and neediness, which caused her to cling to Ted. She couldn't stand to be apart from him. She wanted to be with him every evening after work, no matter what he was doing—laundry, housecleaning, caring for his son in joint custody with his ex-wife, or simply hanging out. It didn't matter to her what mundane thing he was doing. She simply didn't know how to be alone and had no desire to do so. She didn't know what to do with herself when she was alone, and saw no reason for it since she had a companion in Ted. She had lived her entire existence dependent upon other people and living with other people, so it was very difficult to be alone through the evenings and the long nights.

Being with a man who showed her attention was the only thing that seemed to abate her deep-seated fears and attempted to satisfy her emotional needs. More times than not, Sara would sit in her apartment and simply be afraid—afraid of the growing darkness outside, afraid of who might be lurking about with the intention of harming her, afraid of going to sleep, and terrified of the evil nightmares that continued to invade the long nights.

The demons who had dwelled around her since youth still plagued her through the night, taunting and wooing her. Sara lived in constant fear each night, leaving her physically exhausted and mentally taxed through the day, further perpetuating her emotional neediness.

On the rare occasion when Ted wanted an evening to himself, Sara took it very personally, convinced that he no longer cared for her and was in reality trying to gently free himself from her. She didn't trust another person to love her or want her legitimately, and she had no clue about balance in relationships. She had little clue about balance in *any* area of her life. She'd never had that mirrored for her.

She would practically beg Ted to hang out with her every night, even when he was simply doing laundry, paying bills, or other chores. Whenever he resisted and insisted on an evening apart, Sara would sit in her apartment, crying, certain that he was pulling away from her for good. She'd try watching TV or reading, and sometimes she was adventurous enough to go out to a movie to consume the hours alone. She didn't want to be with anyone as much as Ted, so she didn't make a very concerted effort to develop friendships.

She spent every waking moment she could with him, outside their forty-hour workweek, because she needed someone to cling to, someone to love her. He had wooed and pursued her, and she had eventually fallen in love with him, and now convinced that she couldn't live happily apart from him.

She didn't know what true love was, how it was supposed to look or operate, or what it truly entailed. To Sara, love meant someone paying enough caring attention to her that she felt worthy and valued. She didn't know that in order to be truly fulfilled, it would have to begin within herself, by loving, nurturing, and accepting herself. Nor did she know that loving another person and being loved in return was far more about commitment and purpose than emotional feelings drawn from another person. She was a bottomless well of need.

Consequently, whenever Ted's attention waned, she'd fall into depths of despair, convinced that he was going to toss her aside. She had quickly grown to be dependent on him to make her happy and satisfied, rather than herself, and now completely and totally immersed in his life.

In stark contrast to her upbringing, she was now living a very secular lifestyle—with Ted. She continued to pray, but had no other behaviors or characteristics that indicated she even knew there was a God. She believed in Him as she always had, and continued to hope in Him to help her, but wasn't living a Godly life. She prayed for whatever need was most prevalent in her life at any given time—be it to hold on to Ted's love, or rid herself of the nightmares that paralyzed her. She didn't walk out her faith by living according to God's principles, designed for her true fulfillment and joy. She didn't know how to follow God any more than she knew how to be without a man. Her spiritual experience to that point in her life had been one she never wanted to repeat, and most certainly never wanted to embrace. She didn't even know to look for a different kind of church experience than the one she had known.

She was aware that there were a lot of different Christian denominations to choose from, but she didn't know that among them were churches who embraced God's love and devotion rather than legalism; nor did she know the true freedom and joy He gives as a Father of unconditional love. Sara's upbringing had narrowed her thinking to equate all churches with strict authority. Church and religion were not at all what Sara wanted. She'd had enough of that growing up! She wanted unconditional, life-lasting love and security. She wanted to be treated with kindness and respect, to have value and purpose, and to live in freedom from oppressive authority. She believed these things only existed through a relationship with another person—a man. She had no foundation that had taught her the truths about love, security, value, wholeness, and independence through a personal relationship with Jesus Christ. The church denomination of her upbringing had not given her the entire, whole truths of who God is, nor how intimately and deeply He loves and is involved in our daily lives. So she clung to Ted in her desperate need and fear, rather than to God. She spent every minute with him that he allowed, and thought she had it *all* when she eventually moved in with him, just months after leaving school.

Sara adopted Ted's friends and his lifestyle as her own. She didn't know the first thing about loving herself, or being independent and fulfilled apart from another person. She no longer had school friends and the close girlfriends she had been raised with in church would never approve of her living with a man, she was convinced. She was truly alone in the world for the first time. She really had little clue as to the kind of lifestyle she was stepping into. It was a rude and scary awakening.

Ted's circle of friends—about ten in all—were close knit and, like Ted, all older than Sara by at least ten years. They all worked together in the state capitol where she had previously worked with Ted, and the group did everything together outside of work. They were all born in the late forties, early fifties, and as teenagers, a vibrant part of the sixties hippie movement immersed in drugs, sex, folk rock, parties, and communal living. Their lifestyle was a continuum of the sixties. It was a foreign and scary world for Sara who had been raised in such a sheltered, intensely fundamental and authoritative environment.

Ted and his friends were all well-educated, middle-class professionals by day, and pot-smoking hippies by night and weekend. They became Sara's new family and embraced her openly and lovingly as one of them. Peace, love—the sixties' mantra—still hummed. She was so much younger, naïve, and tiny, they were all protective of her and didn't see their lifestyle as one that she needed to be protected from.

As common as cooking dinner and eating it, they rolled joints and smoked pot. They introduced her to all the various ways to "take a toke," or a "hit," from all sorts of paraphernalia of the "pot" world. She became very good at it all. Their use of drugs and alcohol wasn't in the vein of getting "trashed" or "wasted" like the partying youth of the sixties, or that is commonly associated today with young adults, but rather in the stratum of casual, middle class, social indulgence—like smoking a cigarette or having a couple of glasses of wine or beer. Still, it was all very new and starkly different from Sara's upbringing. There had been an incident where Matt, as a teenager, had been caught—by their daddy—trying a cigarette. Matt was beat to near death that night by their daddy. Even the talk of such things as alcohol and cigarettes was taboo. There was certainly never any talk about drugs.

By experience, she learned just how much pot she could smoke to avoid feeling "wasted" and the frightening paranoia that could sneak up on her from too many hits. And she learned the hard way how much alcohol she could drink without making herself sick with a hangover—occasionally for days after. She wasn't at all interested in being out of her head or losing control with the use of drugs and alcohol—she *needed* and desired to have full control over her life. She never again wanted to be controlled by anything or anybody. She simply wanted the calm effect that these substances afforded her with regulated use. She had lived twenty years in daily, high anxiety, so the controlled use of marijuana and alcohol was a very appealing alternative.

In addition to social drinking and pot smoking, Sara was introduced to social cocaine use, as well—a highly addictive drug. Later in life, she would realize even more how God's protective hand had been on her. She was cajoled into trying cocaine at every opportunity the drug drifted into their circle. Not knowing how the drug might adversely affect her, and wanting nothing that might make her lose control over her mind or body, she was fearful and reluctant to try it. She was eventually so persuaded to participate, she relented. Amazingly, and highly uncommon, she felt no effects from the drug whatsoever. She might as well have been snorting powdered sugar, which probably would have given her more of a high than the cocaine had. It simply did nothing for her. She didn't understand what the big deal was about using the popular drug, but saw for herself how it affected those around her who were casually participating. The group was equally surprised that she experienced no high—no effect whatsoever—from the addictive drug, as they all did, especially because she was so tiny and couldn't even take an adult dosage of cold medicine without it knocking her out for an entire day! They were truly puzzled, as was she.

Cajoling from the group prompted her to try cocaine

whenever they got their hands on some, but mercifully and supernaturally, the drug never had any effect on her. She didn't realize until much later in life that God had protected her from substances that are so easily and devastatingly addictive, devouring, debilitating, and destroying. *Once used—cocaine and other drugs—there is often no turning back, no recovery, without intensive, rehabilitative intervention and a lifetime of battling against anaconda strength addiction.*

Just as God had had His protective hand on her spirit and mind throughout her childhood, He graciously veiled her again with unusual protection against addictions. He faithfully preserved her for the future He had destined for her—in spite of her ignorant and very dangerous play at casual mental and physical self-sabotage.

Like marijuana, sexual adventure was also a huge part of the lifestyle that Sara was now entangled. Ted pursued and persuaded her deeper into pornography and all manner of sexual pursuits. She hated it all and she feared it all. This was not the lifestyle she had longed for.

In her heart, she was dying all over again. The freedom she had gained by escaping her dad was exchanged for a different kind of prison. She wanted out, but she was highly entangled emotionally and didn't know how to begin to disentangle from that lifestyle. She got sucked deeper and deeper into darkness—by no one's choice but her own. She simply had not yet fully realized that she had the power to make her own choices and to change her life for the better.

Ted's life was now Sara's. Who he was, who he knew, what he

did, and what he wanted, dictated her every move. She no longer had her own family. Allie was still living out of state, and she had no more contact with her brothers—thanks to her dad.

After Allie had called him the previous year and told him to never again contact Sara, she had still maintained phone contact with her mother. Occasionally, Sara would surprise her mother by showing up at her office to spend the lunch hour with her, or just to chat for a few minutes. She shared the details of her new life with her mother in those clandestine moments, but never talked with her dad, nor saw him. When Sara made the choice to move in with Ted, she naturally shared the news with her mother, who promptly passed the shocking information on to Sara's dad, without her knowledge.

Her mother felt it was wrong, as a wife, to keep information from her husband—even if her husband was proven to be abusive, obsessive, volatile, mentally ill, and irrational. Feeding him a stream of information about Sara's life, not only placed Sara in further jeopardy with her unstable dad, but also was once again another betrayal by her mother. Her mother again proved a greater allegiance to her husband than protection of her daughter.

The news of Sara "living in sin" ignited her daddy's self-righteous fury. He lashed out the wages of sin to Sara's mother and her three brothers, still living at home, called Sara a whore to her family, then, ironically, said she was no longer his daughter. Finally, he mandated to Sara's mother and brothers that they were to have no more contact with her.

After all the sins *he* had committed against her, he was renouncing her?! If that wasn't so pathetically the pot calling the kettle black, it would have been laughable. But it wasn't laughable to Sara, at all. It was another devastating blow from her dad, vicariously received through her mother, to prove that he still held the power. It was more of his self-piousness and another excuse to further exercise control over his family—and hurt Sara.

He had never once taken responsibility or owned up to Sara all the years of abuse and neglect he had consciously chosen against her. Disowning her because of the poor choices she was making as a direct result of *his sins* against her was utterly ludicrous! She wasn't surprised, but nevertheless heartbroken when her mother again chose him over her daughter—as she always had. She had stood up for Sara only once, in Sara's darkest hour, only to turn around and betray her shortly thereafter by siding with him to bring Sara back into that house of Hades.

Chapter Seventeen

At twenty-three, Sara married Ted in a small, outdoor ceremony with only their closest friends to witness. Everyone loved him. He was the life of the party. But when the parties were over, and it was just Sara and he alone, he was not so nice anymore. He constantly ridiculed her, told her she was ugly, and other choice humiliations. She had allowed him to begin to rule her, just as her dad had. Though she took far more freedom with Ted than she was ever allowed under her dad, she was nonetheless in emotional captivity—a prisoner again.

She was determined that no one would ever have reign over her like her dad had, or live a life under a man's abusive authority again—as her mother chose to—so she constantly stood up to Ted. She fought against his attempts to impose derisive authority over her. Standing up to him, against his ugliness toward her, pushed him to greater anger; but that was solely his own choice and not her responsibility—just like her actions and reactions were her own choice.

His verbal abuse gradually progressed to physical abuse, and still she stood up to him, his 6'3", 250 pounds to her 5', 96 pounds. Their relationship grew more and more volatile and frightening for Sara, but like her own mother, she was far too insecure and needy to have the courage to leave him—yet.

By her twenty-fifth birthday, her marriage had quickly deteriorated. Ted was seeing other women, even flaunting his attraction to them right in front of Sara's face. This was terribly deflating, humiliating, and hurtful to Sara, destroying what little self-worth may have remained in her. She was very ripe for the temptation to have an affair when the opportunity presented itself. She again made a self-destructive choice. The affair lasted for several months. Her body was of little value except to gain the temporary fix of feeling worth something.

One night, Sara awoke in the middle of the night, feeling like she'd been hit by a Mac truck and starving for bacon and eggs. She got up and headed to the kitchen. Her breasts felt like lead weights and ached badly. As she devoured breakfast in the middle of the night, she suspected only one thing—pregnancy.

Having her own child was one of her strongest heart's desires, but also terrifying. She loved children and mothering, though. She had always been drawn to children, and they loved her in return. As early as sixteen, she had sought out and embraced every opportunity to work with children— giving piano lessons, teaching Sunday school, directing the children's choir at church. She was pulled to children like a magnet, and they to her. But she was terrified of pregnancy, afraid of the changes that were taking place in her body, afraid of the inevitable labor and delivery, and afraid of the grave responsibility of caring for a new life. She was living in an unhealthy and unstable environment, in a precarious marriage. How could she raise a child in that kind of environment to be all that he could be?

She had been in counseling for quite some time because of the dramatic, adverse affects her childhood was having on her as an adult. In addition, she knew the statistics. More often than not, children who are abused become abusers unless they seek help to understand and change their behavior patterns that result from abuse. She learned that the abused either become prominently *covert* or *overt* abusers, as she has termed the two. She had grown to become a covert abuser, a self-abuser, from as early as she could remember. The thought terrified her that she might also have within her the potential to abuse a child—even though she longed to gather up all the children in the world who were unwanted, abused, or neglected and shelter and shower them with love, care, and protection.

She determined early on in her marriage that the generational curses would end there, with her, and not be passed on to her children and theirs to come. Neither her covert abuses, nor any possible overt abuses that might be lying dormant in her, would be passed to her children or theirs to come. She would do everything possible to end the cycle of abuse.

As she examined her own childhood and made the conscious decision to not allow generational curses to continue, she also looked at the reality of other children presently in abusive homes. She knew that she not only had a desire and responsibility to stop potential abuse within herself, but also to stop abuse everywhere. These two decisions prompted her to go through training to become a volunteer with the state's agency for the prevention of child abuse and neglect, located in the capitol city where she lived and worked.

Her specific training was for what they titled as a "Volunteer Lay Therapist." As a lay therapist, it was Sara's job to make home visits to families who were under the supervision of Social Services for suspected abuse and neglect. As she entered a home and began to visit with the caregiver, it was her job to also assess the children, looking for any signs of neglect and abuse. She would also assess the family's living environment for things that might pose danger to the children. She would share parenting tools with the caregivers, predominately stay-at-home moms, and answer questions that would aid them in healthy and balanced parenting. It was fulfilling work, with the hope that she might be making a difference in a child's life, but it was also emotionally and mentally difficult, time-consuming work. She was spurred on by her desire to do whatever she could to help prevent other children from suffering the horrors she had. Sara knew that abuse on all levels, in all places, must end. It must!

In addition to her work as an advocate for abused and neglected children, Sara worked full-time as the director of a large, early childhood education center. She enjoyed the administrative end of running the center, but she most loved interacting with the children. It was heart-warming and fulfilling, but also occasionally heart wrenching. It was far more than just a job to her—it was love, giving, caring.

There were times when she became too attached to a child, especially to one whose life subtly skirted along the lines of neglect. Fortunately, she witnessed no signs of abuse. The children's quick smiles, uninhibited innocence, and natural laughter rang priceless and heart filling within Sara. She harbored the dream of someday having an orphanage where children would know the joy and freedom of unconditional love and true caring, in a healthy and balanced environment.

In tandem with her work at the center and her volunteer work for the agency, she taught piano in the evenings and on weekends. She had used her extensive piano education background and opened a studio for children ages six to twelve. After a full day of running the center, she'd sprint home to a list of eager young students scheduled for lessons through the evening. The children and her work brought Sara great joy and fulfillment, knowing she was making some positive contributions, no matter how small, in their tender hearts and lives. The children loved her in return with complete abandon.

Despite her faltering marriage, all she was involved in and all she was dealing with internally and externally, she was elated over her pregnancy. She knew she would be a good, loving, and attentive mommy, and that she would protect her baby with her life and pour good things into him (or her).

Yes, Sara had a lot on her plate. Furthermore, she didn't know who the father of her child was—her estranged husband's or her lover's. She suspected in her heart that her baby belonged to her lover and, though she worried over this, she concluded that in the end all that truly mattered was the kind of mother she would be to her child.

She knew she would be raising her baby pretty much alone, without much assistance from Ted. She had tried and tried—everything she knew to try—to make their marriage work, but their foundational beliefs, values, goals, and desires in life, were polar opposite. Out of sheer neediness and immaturity, she had made another huge life mistake by partnering with him.

She had believed—hoped—in "happily ever after" once she had gotten away from her dad, but life was proving her grossly wrong and naive. Her naiveté began to fall from her like brittle autumn leaves exposed to the harsh winds of reality—the reality that life would never offer her a fairytale existence. She had yet to learn that true, abiding happiness and fulfillment does not come from another person, but originates from within by way of knowing and loving one's self for the unique person God created her to be, and through a personal relationship with God, through Jesus Christ.

She was just a young, tender tree in the autumn of this journey of discovery that would slowly evolve through the seasons of her life. Through harsh, cold winters, segueing into the respite and renewal of spring, to the fullness and warmth of summer, she would eventually grow into a strong and sturdy tree—an "Oak" of Isaiah 61:3:

> *He has sent me to bind up the brokenhearted,*
> *   to proclaim freedom for the captives and release*
> *from darkness for the prisoners,*
> *   to proclaim the year of the LORD's favor and the*

day of vengeance of our God,
*   to comfort all who mourn, and provide for those*
who grieve—
*   to bestow on them a crown of beauty instead of ashes,*
*   the oil of gladness instead of mourning,*
*   and a garment of praise instead of a spirit of despair.*
*   They will be called oaks of righteousness, a planting*
*   of the* LORD *for the display of his splendor.*

She was at step one, the shedding of her tender young leaves, the old ways of thinking and believing, to make way for new growth that would someday be the full, strong, and healthy oak that would offer shelter and life to other young, budding trees.

It was devastating for her to realize that life held no "happily ever after" as she had hoped. It raised many questions within her about life and purpose. She was stripped bare of her leaves of false hopes and dreams as the winter winds of reality began to blow stronger through her life.

Chapter Eighteen

Sara was a major workaholic—added to the pregnancy and a near-death marriage. Busyness is one way survivors of abuse *avoid* dealing with all the garbage festering inside them, churning and rotting.

She was still having horrific nightmares that would make Stephen King look like Disney—evil, sadistic, horrifying dreams that would awaken her in the night, terrified and disbelieving of how such horrors could be generated within her own mind. And she was still being awakened in the night between the hours of midnight and 3:00 a.m. by the demons still dwelling around her since childhood.

At that time in her life, Sara didn't know that countless others were living with similar dark spirits around them, and that only God, through the fervent prayers of Godly men and women, could free her and others like her who lived with this.

If you were to research Satanic practices and rituals active in our world today, you would learn that the height of this activity takes place between midnight and 3:00 a.m. It's no coincidence, but rather profound, that at the hour of Jesus' death on the cross, historically calculated to be noon, the sun was black from noon until 3:00 p.m., as if it were midnight.

Satan, demons, and the spiritual world are very real and active at this very moment. The Word of God declares the presence and activities of Satan, demons, and demon possession. It's not some obscure thing or scary fairytale, nor limited to centuries past. There are countless people, right now, who are active in demonic practices and worship. There are many who are possessed, and many who are not possessed but suffering with the presence of demons around them, taunting, wooing, and plaguing them.

Please hear this: When you innocently pursue or allow your children to pursue in the name of fun or curiosity the activities related to the spiritual world—like Ouija boards, Tarot cards, magic spells, séances, horror movies, witchcraft books, etc.—you are opening the door wide for demons to come and dwell around you, and given that open door, they will pursue and woo and taunt in an effort to devour and destroy. This is not pretend stuff. It's very real, very prevalent, and very powerfully at work—right now.

Sara knows this as well as she knows how to eat and breathe. Don't go there! Don't allow your children to go there. Don't open those doors of evil and destruction, bondage and ruin. Leave it alone! Stay in the protective light and presence of the one true and living God, whose love and light dispels all evil and brings true freedom, hope, peace, and joy. The true "happily ever after."

With the massive burdens on Sara's shoulders and in her heart, coupled with the years of childhood abuse and trauma, her adrenal system had become seriously overtaxed. Adverse chemical and hormonal changes had been taking place in her body through the years of trauma, preventing a necessary balance. It was a miracle she was even able to conceive a child.

Sara passed through the early months of pregnancy with good reports and normal test results. Her baby was growing and moving. The only physical problems she experienced outside the normal morning sickness and fatigue were frequent panic attacks causing her to hyperventilate. This lowers necessary carbon dioxide and constricts blood flow.

She had worked very hard to keep her nervousness and anxiety inside so others would see her only as she longed to be—confident, secure, together. She pulled this charade off rather well—most of the time. But, she was still easily sick to her stomach and quick to vomit from anxiety—now coupled with morning sickness. And she still lived with terrible stomach cramps and diarrhea. Now, adding to her distress, she was terrified of the changes that were taking place in her body from the pregnancy.

Ted wasn't much comfort to her and really had not wanted another child, but he wasn't completely against it. He had agreed early on that they could try to have children because Sara was adamant in her desire to be a mother. He was only casually supportive once she became pregnant. He neither shared her excitement nor her fears. He showed little concern for her emotions where it pertained to her pregnancy. She had never been pregnant before and wasn't around anyone else who was. She was alone and frightened in that as well.

The greatest fear that plagued her mind daily, often hourly, was the impending delivery of her baby. Even though she had endured much physical pain in her life, the thought of her body being ravaged and ripped in labor and delivery (as she'd witnessed on TV and read in books), naturally terrified her. These fears served only to prompt and feed her panic attacks.

The week of Thanksgiving, 1985, Sara was at the beginning of her second trimester. Early in the week she had a doctor's appointment and watched her baby in amazement as the technician ran the sonogram wand across her belly to find just the right pose for the picture she would take home. She had learned from an earlier visit that she was having a boy. At that point in development he was fully formed—moving, kicking, swallowing, sleeping, waking… and could hear Sara's voice. She planned to name her boy after her youngest brother, Wayne. They had shared such a close relationship through the years.

In awe, she watched as her baby raised his tiny arm and let it float back down as if saying, "Hi, Mommy." Then everything changed in that moment. There was no more movement. The technician could no longer find the heartbeat. Puzzled, the technician went to find the doctor. A few minutes later, two doctors appeared, probing around her belly in search of the heartbeat and to prompt activity in her baby. There was none. Her tiny, baby boy whom she already loved and anticipated had raised his little arm to her in farewell. He had gone to meet Jesus, right there under her gaze.

That devastating week, when the world around her was giving thanks, Sara had lost the one thing in life she most wanted—her own child to love. Her inconsolable loss made her question what she had to be thankful for and the worth of living. She felt as though her entire life had been unusually cruel. It had; she was right. Losing her baby, coupled with the precarious state of her marriage and facing the demons of her childhood day in and day out was her end. Everything she had been dealing with in life came to a head on that grievous day as they wheeled her into surgery to take her baby's lifeless body from her own.

All the years of abuse and terror, all the struggles and suffering of her present life, coupled with the loss of her baby— for no medical reason the experts could find—drew Sara back down into the slimy pit of hopelessness and despair. There was nothing in life worth living for. Whatever dignity, self-worth, self-respect, purpose, and hope had been lingering was destroyed. She no longer cared about life or living.

Life had died inside her, literally and figuratively, when her baby's spirit was drawn to heaven.

Her counselor consoled and encouraged her as best she could over the ensuing weeks as the year drew to an end, but it was little help. In the end, she felt it would be beneficial for Sara to enter a psychiatric wellness center for a few days, to rest and recuperate emotionally while receiving daily counseling, support, and 'round the clock care. There was a beautiful, contemporary facility right there in town. Sara tentatively agreed. Getting away from everything and everybody for a few days seemed like a fair idea. Despite her devastating low and desire to give up on life, she truly wasn't ready to die yet, but at the same time, she felt no reason to live.

With her husband in tow, sharing concern for her emotional well-being, they arrived at the center of Sara's own free will. She had not been coerced into anything, although she had been strongly encouraged by her therapist that it would allow her the time, space, and care that she desperately needed toward healing. Nevertheless, the thought of going into a mental health center as an in-patient naturally caused her trepidation, though she didn't disagree that it would probably be the most helpful thing at that time.

Once there, with each step toward the entrance, Sara became increasingly uncertain about her decision, but her therapist had already arranged for her stay, and it didn't seem right to not follow through. Still, she began to question what she had committed herself to. Rapid concerns began to gather and swirl in her head as she completed and signed the necessary admission papers at the front desk, acknowledging that she was entering under her own cognizance.

The ink was barely dry on the papers when a female attendant appeared at her side and gently encouraged her to tell her husband good-bye. She did, somewhat reluctantly, and began to follow the attendant across the lobby to a nearby inner door. Sara looked back over her shoulder at Ted, her anxiety growing with each step toward the unknown.

When they reached the door, the kind attendant stopped and turned to her. Further unease grew as she explained to Sara that before they proceeded further—to get Sara settled into her room—she would need to relinquish anything sharp that she had in her purse and luggage—fingernail file, clippers, scissors, razor. She suddenly felt like a prisoner being led away to her permanent cell.

In naive surprise, and with growing alarm at having to relinquish some of her personal effects, she asked, "Why?" The attendant gently smiled and explained that it was for Sara's safety, so she would not harm herself.

Alarm growing to near panic, Sara nodded her understanding and began to dig through her purse, blinded by gathering tears. Everything on the attendant's verbal list was common, ordinary items Sara had taken for granted. Simple tools of hygiene for their intended use now took on a whole new look, foreign in concept to Sara—weapons of self-abuse. Handing them over, the attendant gave her a warm smile of assurance as she held open the door.

As the door quietly closed behind her, frenzied thoughts flooded Sara's mind that perhaps she had been too quick in agreeing to this plan. What if, in reality, she would never be allowed to leave? What if she was being locked away forever in one of those ghastly insane asylums like she'd seen in TV movies? Had that gentle smile on the attendant's face in reality been a knowing smile of pity, thinking Sara to be psychotically naive?

She envisioned all sorts of horrible experiments "they" would perform on her. She hoisted in her mind the muted sounds of blood curdling screams of "crazy" people echoing through the hallways from distant rooms. She pictured helpless bodies trapped in straightjackets "for their own protection," and long needles carrying drugs that would halt their ability to ever again think for themselves, diminishing their acuity to escape.

She'd end up like "them." She began to panic. In her mind, she saw lifeless bodies shuffling slowly along the corridors, carrying the vague look of the insane in their eyes, hair unkempt, faces pale and vacant. She saw bare legs exposed through slits in the back of gaping, Velcro gowns as the captives made their way to nowhere, as if sleepwalking, too deranged to recognize their own demise.

What have I agreed to? What have I done by voluntarily committing myself?! *What's going to happen to me?* Her mind agitated and raced. She trusted no one. She couldn't. Yes, the attendant had been awfully kind—just like the ones she had seen in those scary asylum movies. Did this person leading her into the bowels of this crazy-house believe her to be crazed?! Was her gentle kindness in reality an act of appeasement, believing Sara did not know or understand that she would be with them for a *very long time*? Did they *all* really think she was crazy—including her therapist and her husband? Was this really a conspiracy between them to get rid of her? Had they arranged all of this behind her back and made her believe she had made her own choice, when all along they had made the choice for her?

Her rapidly growing paranoia kicked her self-preservation tools into high gear and dictated that she hide her fear from whomever held the power over her and her future. She knew how to pretend and deceive in order to avoid punishment and survive. She would suck up her fears, not show her panic, and play it *cool* so they wouldn't see her as a potential threat and shoot her up with some mind-altering drug. She had to remain lucid if she was going to devise a clever way to renege on this *temporary* stay. If she got all emotional and showed her *true* fear and paranoia, they would surely think her mad and perhaps even bind *her* in a straight jacket! If she suddenly gave way to her panic, paranoia, and fear, they would be *convinced* she belonged there with all the other crazy people, and lock her away for good.

What have I done?! Her mind raced into deeper suspicion as she searched for the best course of action to convince "them" that she was actually very normal and quite capable of leading a productive life in society—without harming herself or others—and that she had made a simple mistake by agreeing to enter the facility. She'd convince them that she didn't need to stay there after all. But, to pull this off, she'd have to put on her best act ever. *I can do this. I can convince them that despite what my husband and therapist may have told them, I'm quite sane and a highly productive member of society.*

She was very good at acting. She'd had a lifetime of daily practice. She determined that she would not reveal anything that "these people" might use against her to certify her as crazy and justify locking her away forever. No matter where she turned in life, she felt that someone was always trying to imprison her. She didn't realize how far from reality she was moving on this journey of alarm. Everything she was thinking and beginning to believe could not have been further from the truth.

It was Friday when she entered the facility and by Sunday afternoon she was insisting that Ted come and get her out of there. He did, that day. None of her fears had materialized; in fact, everyone had been kind and caring, yet she had worked herself into such a state of paranoia, she *had* to know by physical action that she was truly free to leave.

Contrary to her paranoia, she had not been a prisoner, and they had not thought her insane. *The abused are not crazy, they are deeply wounded.* The abused don't need a crazy house; they need a truly caring house.

It had not been a crazy house she had entered. If she had been honest with herself and more trusting in those who had her best interest at heart, she would have known that she was in good hands, with good people who had dedicated themselves to help her to regain her footing. But life had taught her to trust no one. She hadn't been able to trust her own parents, and every man she trusted in life had failed her. Going into a facility, even of her own free will, had simply *felt* too much like another prison; too confining, so it was the best thing for her to leave and return home.

Her therapist was naturally very concerned about her. Sara promised her that she would take it easy, not go back to work for several weeks, rest and grow stronger, and would continue to see her several times a week. Sara kept her promises.

By the New Year, she was feeling physically stronger and

less emotional; however, she felt no better about her marriage, and still grieved the loss of her baby. Her marriage continued to decline and with more heartache. Sara was desperately alone and desperate to cling to someone. She began to spiral out of control, giving her body away to every man who showed an interest in her. It was not *at all* about sex—far to the contrary—Sara could totally do without sex. It was all about feeling loved, wanted, and valued as a human being.

She no longer cared about life. She no longer cared about herself, her body, or her dignity. She had grown to have less and less value for herself. She was still frantically—hopelessly—seeking things that could not be attained from others. Things that could only be gained from within, once she understood certain truths—who God had created her to be and how unique and valuable she was, simply because she had been born.

At twenty-seven, she had slept with more men than she dared count and felt what it must feel like to live the life of a prostitute. The only difference was that she received no monetary compensation, only a temporary emotional fix that left her feeling more and more worthless, needy, and dying.

Is this it? She asked herself in despair. *Is this all there is to life? Is heartache and suffering all I have to look forward to? Does everyone else live as lonely and depressed? Does anyone really, truly care for another person? Is there anyone who can be trusted? Is there anyone who will just love me for me?* She concluded not, and surmised that this was why she had heard so many woeful songs on the radio of love gone wrong, hopelessness, and despair. *Does God truly care?* She continued to cry out. *Or has He given up on me because I've broken all the rules?*

Without a hint of doubt, she believed there was a God

and still believed in "once saved, always saved." She didn't doubt that she had truly accepted Jesus into her heart at age thirteen and that her name was written in the "Lamb's book of life" (Revelation 21:27). She believed in the whole truths of God's Word—not because the truths (in part), had been drilled into her mind and repeatedly hammered in place since her birth. She believed for herself alone because she had spent time with God and had read for herself what had been taught and believed through centuries of Christianity, beliefs that a myriad of men and women had died for through the ages. If countless people had given their lives for the sake of the written Word of God, and endless other lives had been drastically changed through the centuries for the better, she had to take a closer look. But apart from all others and all else, she instinctively and inherently knew that nature, in which she found such hope, peace, joy, and wonder, was *far* too complex and intricate to *not* have had an ultimate, supreme, intelligent Creator.

She witnessed all around her, daily, a Creator who was passionate about color, beauty, texture, smell, taste, sound, and *life*, a Creator who had an enormous and captivating humor. She was in constant amazement of the sky, the vast, vast universe, delicate flowers and imposing, towering trees, ice-cold and boiling hot natural springs, lush forests brimming with life … and on and on.

She was stunned by the fact that all music ever created comes from seven, basic tones, and all color variations from only three primary colors. She was elated and impassioned over the unique taste of a fresh, ripe peach, banana, and kiwi, of cocoa beans which could produce chocolate, cow's milk, so refreshing and thirst-quenching, which could be transformed into the amazing texture and taste of ice cream—her favorite indulgence.

Creation was simply … *stunning*. There was no doubt of a supreme Creator—God.

Sara couldn't look at an insect or an animal without thinking how this highly passionate and intelligent Creator must have also possessed a great, deep, booming soul-laugh when He fashioned the zebra, giraffe, and monkey, and that His heart swelled with love and amusement over the panda and penguin that He brought to life. There was no doubt that He—God—was deeply in love with *all* His creation. Even more mind-awakening and stunning than creation, so vast, intricate, and incredible, is what she read in His word about how He loves mankind *even more* than all else He has created, and that He created *all things,* too vast for understanding, specifically for humankind to enjoy and care for. Wow!

He drives home this fact to us in the most profound and ultimate act of love—sending His only son, His only child, to die a horrifying death as the ultimate sacrifice, so that every man, woman, and child would no longer be separated by sin from the all-knowing, righteous, and Holy Creator. Through this ultimate and final sacrifice, she knew that every man, woman, and child could have the assurance of eternal hope, of completeness of love and joy, simply by accepting—in simple faith—the *free gift* of His son's sacrifice. Wow!

Sara knew there was an amazing Creator, the one true and living God, a God who listens and speaks, cares and loves, and participates intimately in our daily lives—a real and perfect Daddy. Without these beliefs, which stemmed from what she had personally experienced on a deep level, there was no point to life, no hope, no joy, no true love. She believed, and she would *always* believe.

But how can He possibly forgive the way I'm living and the things I've done—against the principals and commands He had instituted specifically for her ultimate joy and protection? She was treating her temple with such callous abandon—the body He created specifically for her to enjoy and experience all He had created for her. She was defiling and devaluing herself by the personal choices she was making.

Sara loathed herself. She loathed her behavior. She loathed her lifestyle and her very life. She knew she wouldn't live to see thirty if she continued to live so recklessly. There was nothing good left in her life. She no longer cared about caring for herself. *What is the point?* She cried, defeated.

Intrinsically, she knew there *had* to be a point. She knew that she carried an unbelievably strong spirit within her that God had created—a spirit that would not, could not relinquish all hope. Hadn't she already survived far worse for years at the hands of evil through her childhood? Had her dream and hope of escaping her dad, coming into freedom and choice, not come true? Wasn't it her own proactive choices that were keeping her in bondage and despair now, rather than someone else—or God? God was not choosing this life for her. He loved her far too much to choose anything less than wholeness, joy, peace, and blessing. Yes ... she was making her own choices now, apart from her dad and his influences, and apart from anyone else. She was the adult now. She was responsible for her own choices now and could not rightly blame him, or God, or anyone else, for the conscious decisions she was making. But, how could she change her life, as needy and weak-willed as she had grown to be?

Sara prayed and longed in her heart for something more, something better, something satisfying, something freeing. She prayed and hoped for a completely different future—somehow. She longed for a husband who would truly love and respect her, treat her with dignity and as an equal, a husband who would share her faith and beliefs in God and His Word—personally as his own—and want to live a pure life seeking Him. She longed for a life free of perverse sex, threats of abuse, demons, nightmares, depression, oppression, and discontentment. She longed for true freedom from all the bondages and oppressions. She longed for wholeness and a loving, Godly family of her own. She longed for a church family of friends who would truly love and nurture her, a church whose beliefs offered hope, freedom, and true joy—not rules, laws, and fear. She longed to live a life of real joy, peace, and contentment. She asked herself time and again, *is there such a life as this?*

She chose to continue to hold to the same truth that had seen her through the dark days of her childhood: "Now faith is being sure of what we hope for and certain of what we do not see" (Hebrews 11:1). She could not see in her future any of the things she longed and prayed for; but she never let go of her hope, or her concrete faith in God, which perpetually regenerated new hope and life within her.

She wept and prayed. Unbeknown to her, God's tears were continually watering the seeds of life buried deep inside her—seeds that were being nurtured by the Spirit living within her and fed by the life-giving manna of His Word that she read, memorized, and clung to. Seeds that were breaking open and giving way to tiny buds of beauty and life, struggling to break free from the darkness and bondage of the heavy soil of sin. Seeds that would, with purpose and determination, eventually push through the darkness to blossom into the full light of a new day—His glory—her new and transformed life.

Chapter Nineteen

Months before her pregnancy and loss, Sara had begun to see her psychologist to help her deal with the years of abuse that were now so directly and adversely affecting her adult life. As she began to unfold her life story, the magnitude of what she had experienced and survived became apparent to her counselor. She not only felt it necessary for Sara to see her more than once each week, but also felt it imperative that Sara join a weekly support group of female survivors of physical, sexual, and emotional childhood abuse.

Sara saw her counselor several times a week, each time pulling out handful after handful of fermenting garbage as she relived and relinquished her past. But revisiting hell rendered her debilitated to move through a normal routine. She was unable to work and eventually made the wise decision to quit her job in order to fully focus on all the work neces-sary to bring her closer to healing and the hope of whole-ness. Her emotional and mental work would be rewarded with *truth*. The truth would indeed make her free, just as the Word of God promised in John 8:32 (KJV), "… the truth shall make you free."

The truths of God, His promises, His characteristics, would fuel Sara's hope and sustain her faith. It would enable her to live life more fully and freely. But it would be *her* choice, a choice only she could make. She could choose to continue in counseling to gain guidance, insight, and tools, and commit to do the hard work necessary to clean out the mounds of garbage rotting inside her, suffocating the life out of her. She could choose to change her behaviors, patterns, and attitudes, and re-train and re-parent herself. She could choose to work toward becoming *all* she knew inside she had the potential to be. Or, she could choose to continue living in fear, grief, injury, defeat, self-loathing, self-abuse, hatred, anger, pain, disillusionment, bondage, debilitation, medioc-rity. She could choose to maintain life in survival mode or *thriver* mode. Bottom line—it was her choice and hers alone. No one could make this life choice for her. Others could only aid and encourage her along the way.

There was no easy road to healing and wholeness, only determination, perseverance, dedication, commitment, and hard work, coupled with hope and faith in God. He was on her side—always had been—but the choices were now hers. In the end, she chose to do the work and to stand on the truths of God's Word, believing His promise that the truth would indeed make her free.

Life always comes down to a choice, not just for Sara, but for each and every one of us. Even when there appears to be no choice, *there is always a choice*, and that choice is yours—alone. The choices won't always be clear, but nevertheless, there's still a choice. The choices won't always be the ones we wish we could have, but still, there's a choice. Regardless of how life, circumstances and people are packaged or perceived, there's always a personal choice—yours!

The time had come for Sara to make some new, better, different, wiser choices.

Sara's counselor and other mental health professionals involved in her care described her as a "walking miracle." Each were amazed that she was so hardworking, motivated, productive, creative, and professional—considering all she had been through and survived, and all she was presently dealing with and assimilating. More often than not, survivors of abuse are debilitated to varying degrees in meeting the day-to-day challenges as a productive adult. They get stuck in the mire or quicksand, fighting for every day, every hour. This assessment of the norm was substantiated for Sara once she began attending the weekly support group.

Every woman in the group lived with varying serious emotional and mental handicaps that greatly impacted their day-to-day lives. Some were suffering from multiple personalities, others schizophrenia, and other serious disorders common to victims of long-term abuses. *Abuse devours and destroys lives.*

It was terribly grievous, tragic, and awakening for Sara to witness the destructive outcome of abuse through these victims—these survivors—she sat in a circle with week after week. She began to see why the professionals over her care were calling her a "walking miracle." She began to realize how miraculously God had protected her mind and spirit from the natural consequences of sins perpetrated against her, and how grave and severe are the implications of physical, sexual, emotional, and spiritual abuse. For the first time, she truly recognized that she was *indeed* a living, breathing miracle, functioning at an amazing level of clarity and capability of mind and spirit that she could only attribute to God's hand. She began to understand that this was solely due to the powerful, supernatural Spirit of God within her, and the life-giving manna of His Word that she carried within her daily—the "Good News" of God's love, mercy, grace, and forgiveness. The good news that God is in the business of transforming lives and setting the captives free. (Isaiah 61) The good news that He is in the business of healing and restoring wholeness, freedom, *and so much more.*

These earliest realizations could hardly compare to the incredible, supernatural promises, purposes, and power that God would reveal in and through Sara in the coming years. It would be an intimate journey between her and God, a journey she would personally choose day by day, month by month, year by year. Her choice.

> "Counsel and sound judgment are mine: I have understanding and power. By me kings reign and rulers make laws that are just, by me princes govern, and all nobles who rule on earth. I love those who love me, and those who seek me find me" (Proverbs 8:14-24).

Chapter Twenty

Early in adulthood, Sara began to experience with regularity a strange phenomenon. She would know things before they happened, through dreams and sudden visions. Whatever prophetic dream or vision came to her, each one came true. She didn't know what to make of this. She didn't seek it out; she couldn't control it. She couldn't make it happen; it just *happened*, time and time again.

When Sara had moved back to her home state and city to be with Ted, she knew it was likely that she would run into her dad somewhere, at sometime, in the city. The thought of running into him terrified her. He still had a powerful, emotional hold over her. She constantly lived looking over her shoulder and peering around every corner, terrified for the day she would come face-to-face with him.

One day, not long after Sara moved back, she was driving through the city and suddenly got the foreknowledge that she was about to see her daddy. It was as if someone was giving her warning in preparation for seeing him. Naturally, she braced herself for the impact. She had not laid eyes on him since he had left her at school long before, nor spoken with him since the day Allie had told him never to contact Sara again. The mere thought of seeing him frightened her. Not a block later, there he was, driving past her in his car. She didn't notice if he had noticed her or not because her mind was captivated by the supernatural that had just taken place in her thoughts, the forewarning. She wasn't sure if she was more frightened from seeing him, or stunned by the fact that she had gotten the foreknowledge and it came true.

Not long after that first incident, the same thing happened again, then again and again. She was still terrified of her dad and began to depend on the forewarnings and take comfort in what she believed to be God giving her these cautions. She began to trust in Him more and more with each prophetic "heads up" He'd give her, always amazed that each one came true. Then, one day, God revealed His supernatural authority in a most significant, powerful, heart-altering way. She'll always remember every detail like it just happened yesterday.

It was during the morning and Sara was busy at work. She suddenly got a very strong, vivid vision and knowledge in her mind that Ted, her husband, was going to be in a serious accident that day, with a large semi trailer truck on the interstate, and be killed. Despite their fragile marriage, Sara never wanted to see Ted harmed and certainly not dead. She not only loved him, but she was greatly concerned that he had not ever asked God into his heart and life. If he died that day, she was not certain that he would enter into eternity to embrace God, but rather he might be separated from Him forever, without hope. The reality of life and death hanging in the balance and the implications of both—death and not knowing Jesus Christ—were terrifying.

Based on the many times Sara had received foreknowledge in the past, she was almost certain that this vision was from God. But, if Ted was truly going to be in a fatal accident, what could she possibly do to stop it? She was frantic. He was, in fact, going to be driving home that very day from a business trip out of town. Sara knew in her heart that this tragedy was in the making and that sometime during the day, Ted would be in an accident with a semi and not survive.

Sara was panicked at the likely reality of this vision and began to pray earnestly. She could not think about work for worrying. She stopped and devoted herself to prayer. She went into the supply closet, closed herself inside, and continued to pray fervently for Ted's safe return. Still, she had no peace. Ted was going to die that day.

She knew she had to go home, leave the distraction of telephones and activity to give her full attention to prayer. She went straight home, knelt down beside her bed and prayed. Still, no peace came. She felt an urgency to enlist another person to pray with her.

One of Sara's aunts was a prayer warrior and dedicated to her belief in the power of the Spirit of God through prayer. She had gone to church with her aunt once, but it was an unusual and uncomfortable experience. Sara had never been in a church that played drums and electric guitars, and sang high-energy praise songs that were not out of the hymnal, or where people raised their arms toward heaven and danced as they sang. She had always been taught that dancing was a sin and that behavior in the church was to be serious and stoic. So, she was pretty confused and skeptical by all the charismatic activity surrounding her in the name of Jesus. But she knew her aunt loved God and prayed with all her might.

Sara called her aunt and together they prayed earnestly over the phone for Ted's safe return. After a lengthy time in prayer, Sara was filled with peace and felt that everything would be all right. Still, she waited somewhat anxiously for Ted's return that evening, and was relieved when she saw him come through the door.

"How was your trip?" She asked him, trying to sound casual and conversational.

"Fine," he replied as courtesy.

I have to know more, she reasoned to herself. *I have to know if anything out of the ordinary happened on the road.* Although she believed the vision had been from God, she still wanted concrete confirmation. She casually continued, "So, it was an uneventful trip, huh?"

"Yeah," he replied, distracted. "Well, I did get a terrible migraine on the way home," he backtracked. Ted was prone to frequent migraines, so this wasn't news to Sara. "It got so bad, I had to pull off the interstate at a rest stop and take a nap," he shared as he puttered around, putting his things away. "It was just as well, though," he shrugged. "I would have just been stuck, sitting on the interstate anyway. When I pulled back on the road, I saw up ahead that there'd been a major accident with a semi."

A chill surged through her body in amazement at how directly the Lord had spoken with her that day. *Thank you, thank you,* she breathed in prayer as her faith soared to new heights. She was grateful for Ted's safety and for the supernatural experience that gave her opportunity to witness firsthand the power of prayer as promised in Matthew 18:19–20, "Again, I tell you that if two of you on earth agree about anything you ask for, it will be done for you by my Father in heaven. For where two or three come together in my name, there am I with them."

Sara was stunned to silence.

This experience not only boosted her faith but also affirmed in her that the promises of God *are* real, and she could count on them. She didn't fully understand this spiritual gift of foreknowledge that God was nurturing within her, but she knew she had been given some kind of gift that kept presenting itself. Because she had always been taught by her church and her dad that the manifestation of the Spirit (often referred to as spiritual gifts), are no longer manifest today, Sara yearned for more understanding in light of the gift she had within her.[7]

She needed to know why scripture said one thing about the manifestations of the Spirit, but so many churches believed and taught that spiritual gifts were limited to the era of the ancient New Testament church. If that were true, she rationalized, how could this recurring gift of prophecy within her be explained? Cracks began to form in the foundation of her upbringing and began to crumble away as God continued to reveal Himself to her and lay a new foundation—truth. She was no longer convinced that she had been taught the complete truths of God's Word.

♥ ♥ ♥

Sara knew her lifestyle and behaviors had grown *way* out of control. She had been allowing and even encouraging men to use her without regard to decency, morals, or values. In a last attempt to try and turn her life and marriage around, she convinced Ted to go to a counselor with her. It became apparent after a handful of sessions that he had no desire whatsoever to change their lifestyle, and Sara was no longer willing to live a lifestyle of sin, abuse, bondage, and oppression. She had to make a difficult and life-changing choice to either stay in her present lifestyle, living out the rest of her days resolute, or to choose to leave that lifestyle for the promise of something better, something freeing, and truly satisfying. *The choice was hers alone,* just like her husband's choice was his alone. She had the free will and power to make choices. *God has given every human being that right, that power, that privilege.* By doing nothing at all, she was still making a choice—the choice to honor man over God.

In 1987, at the age of twenty-seven, Sara made the decision to leave Ted and all that their life together had represented. She chose to move back to the state where Allie and her husband and children still lived, where the two of them had attended college. Her sister had always been there for her, no matter the choices Sara made. Her three brothers had been there for her in spirit while still confined under their dad's authority, and later had always there for her in person, loving her and supporting her decisions. Likewise, her two closest friends that she had gained during her marriage to Ted—Kaye and Donna—had both stood by her, too, no matter her highs and lows, good decisions or bad, and have remained her life-friends. None of them ever turned their backs to Sara, just as God never turned His back to her.

This was the beginning of dawn in Sara's life—a new day—as she began to make many other positive life choices that would move her toward becoming the woman God had purposed her to be long before the day she was born. She had always *felt* inside that she had so much more potential than she was tapping into, so much more to offer. She felt that the woman she was, or could be, had been barricaded, imprisoned within concrete walls inside her. The walls of her inner prison began to crumble on the day she realized she had the power to make her own choices, and that it was her choice alone to work to completely destroy those walls and be completely freed from the power she had allowed others to have over her.

Chapter Twenty-One

When she met and began to get to know the man who would eventually become her second husband, she realized how God had answered her prayers once again. Greg possessed many of the qualities she had longed for and prayed for in a life-companion. He mirrored her own hunger for the deeper things of God, and the desire to make Him center of their lives. He was a man of integrity and honesty and proved that he truly wanted to know Sara as a whole person. Since the day they met, he treated her with a great deal of respect and dignity and displayed a genuine appreciation and encouragement for her gifts and dreams. Greg loved Sara despite all the evils, influences, and choices of her past, just as Allie, her brothers, Kaye, and Donna had—and just as God always had. Her valley of diamonds (from her prophetic childhood dream), was now materializing before her eyes. "... the great, priceless, limitless treasury of beautiful and brilliant people Sara would amass along her life journey. Strong, loving, caring people ever before her, in her line of vision ... "

Early in their relationship, Sara and Greg chose to become active in church together. Both sought to learn more about prayer, hearing God's voice, and seeking His will for their lives, individually and as a couple.

One year after they met, they married. A month later, they were ecstatic to be expecting their first child, near Sara's thirtieth birthday. She was on cloud nine and constantly thanked God for handcrafting a husband specifically for her and for the many blessings she now had in her life.

Have they messed up along the way? You bet! Was Sara a challenge for Greg with all she needed to work through, and work toward? Certainly. But God was always faithful, forgiving, gracious, and loving, who "... works out everything in conformity with the purpose of his will, in order that we ... might be for the praise of his glory" (Ephesians 1:11–13).

As difficult as life could too often be, they individually and as a couple continued to hang on to their faith and hope in God, and strive to live a life of purpose and peace that could only come from an intimate relationship with their Creator, God.

Sara was finally in an environment where she could truly begin to heal, but the struggles inside her were far from over. She continued to have constant, horrific nightmares that would render her to hot tears of hatred, injustice, and consuming fear. Since the onset of their marriage, her cries in the night would awaken Greg several times a week. He would comfort her, hold her and care for her, showing her how much she was loved.

She now had a wonderful, loving, Christian husband who supported her through the hard and tiring work of recovery and renewal. Greg was there as she struggled to overcome the various physical and emotional debilitations caused by a lifetime of childhood abuses and neglect. It was a long and arduous journey for them both, but in different ways. It was a path they individually chose and committed to take together—she toward recovery and Greg toward encouraging her with commitment, patience, kindness, grace, and love. She knew the potential she had and remained resolute to learn how to no longer allow her past to rule and shape her daily choices and thus her future, her own personal destiny— and their future as husband and wife and parents.

Driven by her deep-seated need to feel worthy and purposed in life, and fueled by her resolve to no longer allow her dad, others, and evil to keep her debilitated and ultimately win the battle, she dedicated herself to change. She resolved to become all that God had created her to be. With unrelenting dedication to spiritual growth through a personal relationship with God, and continued education in her three primary areas of passion—music, writing, and graphic design—she was afforded the blessing of success in all four.

Her staunch devotion toward becoming *all* that God had created her to be spiritually, mentally, and emotionally against the odds, in the face of her on-going, daily battle against the natural consequences of her past, was a personal *choice*. She cannot take for granted the blessings of these achievements, but daily sits in awe of the supernatural power of God available to each and every one of us who makes the personal choice with determination to apply His principles and claim His promises. It doesn't matter your past, how you've suffered at the hands of others, or the poor choices you've made in life, you *can* rise above the past and truly become *all* that God has purposed and destined you to be with determination and dedication.

❤ ❤ ❤

In hand with continual nightmares, she would often be awakened at 2:00 a.m. with the presence of demons still around her, adding to her fears. She got into the habit of praying herself to sleep every night (and still does to this day), but the nightmares and demons continued to plague her night after night, year after year, though they were slowly diminishing as she progressed in her spiritual journey and moved closer to healing and wholeness.

As part of her dedication toward becoming *all* God had created her to be, Sara continued to see a counselor to assist in her determination to heal from her past. It was an ongoing course of perseverance, hard work, prayer, and seeking God. She was now surrounded by sincerely loving, Godly people who made their own personal choices to encourage her, pray for her, and persuade her further toward healing and reaching her potential.

She and Greg had located a wonderful, vibrant body of believers who proactively practiced small group communities functioning outside the church walls. Weekly, the small groups met in various homes for fun, Bible study, prayer, reflection, and relationship building. When a member of the group was sick, or needed a hand, the group pitched in without reserve, invested time and love to meet practical needs.

Their group was a mixture of young adults, middle aged, seniors, singles, married, and divorced. Each person offered a refreshing, insightful, and challenging view of life's day-to-day struggles and achievements. Sara and Greg deeply loved and valued the diverse group who truly became family to one another.

Week after week of sharing individual challenges and joys brought a sturdy confidence and security to the group that ensured they were all journeying through life together—as a team, a family—who could truly depend on one another. They learned to love and listen without condition—no matter what was shared or what transpired in someone's life. It was an amazing time of spiritual growth through the week, arm in arm with powerful corporate worship, teaching, and community, on Sunday mornings when the whole church body gathered together.

Pastor James and his wife, Laura, were sincere, attentive, warm, and caring leaders, advisors, and friends, who saw the value, purpose, and potential in those they had the privilege to serve. They recognized, embraced, and encouraged the gifts and potential in Sara and Greg. Neither had ever experienced such genuine care and concern from pastoral leadership. It was life-giving and restoring.

Pastor James was also a profound and prolific teacher. Impassioned to dig deep into the Word, he challenged Sara and Greg weekly to deep reflection and enriched their hearts to serve God and others according to God's principles for life and living. It was the first time Sara or Greg was actually eager for church each Sunday morning!

They thrived under Pastor James and Laura's loving care, coupled with the intimate care of their small group and church body. They prayed for Sara and Greg, and encouraged them as Sara continued to persevere and work through all the years of abuse toward healing, wholeness, and freedom from the debilitations that still bound her. They never failed Sara. They stuck by her, loved her unconditionally, picked her up when she fell, cheered her on when she was weary, and proved—contrary to what Sara had believed—that there *are* indeed churches and believers who speak the whole truths of God's Word and practice His freeing love, grace, mercy, forgiveness, accountability, joy. Her valley of diamonds had expanded greatly.

It was truly an incredible peak in Sara and Greg's spiritual and whole-life journey. This period of time in their lives gave Sara the second wind to continue the race set before her—to reach that growing light at the end of the corridor, push through the door to true freedom and restoration, and become *all* that God had created her to be.

> *I consider my life worth nothing to me,*
> *if only I may finish the race*
> *and complete the task the Lord Jesus has given me—*
> *the task of testifying to the gospel of God's grace.*

Acts 20:24

♥ ♥ ♥

One morning, their three-year-old son, Scott, came into the kitchen where Sara was busy at the counter and asked impatiently, "Mommy, why does that man keep bothering me?" She whirled around to him in alarm, with the panicked thought that a strange man would be standing there in her kitchen.

"What man?" She gaped, looking around. All manner of thoughts invaded her mind as alarm bells sounded in her head.

"That man that comes into my room at night," he replied factually. "He won't leave me alone." He was clearly perturbed, but distracted by the snacks she'd placed on the table for him.

A dawning gripped Sara's heart as she considered that one of the demons who had been ever-present around her was now manifesting himself visibly to her son. This was acutely serious and Sara quickly grew angry as the reality of generational curses came to mind. She determined then and there, standing in her kitchen, staring at her beautiful, blonde-headed boy, that the generational curses that had been passed to her would *stop* with her, today. They would end with her and not plague her children or theirs to come, knowing that " ... now is the day of salvation" (2 Corinthians 6:2). Now was the day of reckoning with evil that God had prophesied to her through her recurring childhood dream. Today was the day to strip evil from her life, her son's life, and their future generations.

She had long before committed to end the cycle of generational abuses, but had never before considered—until that morning—the generational curses of spiritual evil passed from generation to generation. Her dad had effectively passed it on to her, and now she was seeing how it would otherwise subtly be passed down to her own children and theirs to come. That must be stopped as well—now—and it was her choice, her responsibility, to be proactive toward that end.

Sara curbed her anger inward as she sat down on the sofa, drew her son protectively close and gently inquired, "Tell Mommy about this man who comes into your room. What does he look like?"

"He's brown." Her precocious three-year-old replied, matter-of-fact. He fiddled with the dinosaurs standing erect in battle on the coffee table before him, reminding her of the spiritual war in which she was engaged.

Sara knew, without a shred of doubt, that it was a demon making his presence known to her son, just as they had hovered around her since childhood, and her daddy before her. *From how many generations back had this present evil come?*

Oh, God…oh, God…oh, God… Sara cried in her heart, weighted down by the gravity of what was happening to her family and the potential destruction being made strikingly evident through her precious boy.

"Where do you see the brown man in your room?" She asked casually but intently, not wanting to alarm him by her fear or anger, lest he take those burdens on himself as well.

"At the end of my bed, and he won't leave me alone," he exclaimed in irritation. He climbed onto the sofa beside her and prepared to leap off. He was an active boy who would far rather fly from the furniture than sit on it.

"What do you mean, he won't leave you alone?" She drew his attention back. "Does he talk to you?" She asked, as fear for her son and protection of him rapidly mounted in her heart.

He leaped and landed on his sturdy, little feet—triumphant. "He says he wants to share my clothes with me," he replied, annoyed. "But I told him I don't want to," rushing on a little more emphatically, now ready to trade this cozy inquisition for his Nerf ball and bat.

Sara knew that the demon telling her son that he wanted to share his clothes was in reality him wanting to take possession of her son—as she felt they had taken possession of her own dad, and had tried to take possession of her, without success. The evil one is persistent, too often enticing and subtle, and very cunning.

Within the hour, she had packed him and some toys in the car and headed to see Pastor James. She and Greg had great respect for him and their church leadership. This wasn't the first time Pastor James had dealt with issues of demonic forces in someone's daily life, and he and Laura knew of Sara's childhood exposures to the spirit world and some of the abuses she'd survived. Real-life spiritual warfare was prevalent among many people, but not often revealed as Sara was courageously doing, taking a stand against evil and curses by acknowledging the truth aloud. Pastor James had had enough experience in helping others to be rid of pestering spirits to know without hesitation how he needed to proceed. He immediately called a number of Godly people from their church to meet at Sara's home that very evening.

The group of prayer warriors, standing strong in the authority of their faith in God, gathered around Sara and Greg, and laid hands on them in prayer. They prayed with authority against the evil dwelling among her family, speaking the power of the name of Jesus and His blood covering. Then they moved into each room of the house, commanding the demons flee outside in the name of Jesus and never return.

After a time of ardent, commanding prayer, Sara and

Greg both felt the lifting of oppression and Sara felt the demons depart from their home. But she still felt their lingering at a distance, outside in their backyard, fierce in their demonic determination to stay attached like bloodthirsty leeches feeding on the fear of those they taunt.

The group traveled outside and continued to pray with authority the blood of Jesus around the property. Sara felt the spirits move outside of her family's sphere of coming and going. It was a whole new level of freedom for Sara and her family.

This freedom—abolishing generational curses—took place in 1993. To this day, Sara's son has never again been bothered by "the brown man," and Sara has never again been awakened in the night by their presence. *Free!*

She was finally beginning to grasp more fully God's all-consuming and incomparable love and power, His mercy, grace, patience, longsuffering, and forgiveness toward her personally. She was beginning to understand and personally own I John 1:9, which promises that, "If we confess our sins, He is faithful and just to forgive our sins and cleanse us from all unrighteousness."

Sara had a lot of sins that she carried on her tiny frame and in her big heart. She not only carried the weight of all the sins *she* had committed against God and others through the years, but also all the sins that had been perpetrated *against* her, first by her dad for nineteen years, then by every man she had allowed to use her. Sara was laden down with sins—her sins and the sins of others against her.

In the fall of 2006, Sara sat and considered the wisdom of I John 1:9 as she sketched her life story in obedience to God's prompting. As she read the words, "our sins," the

Spirit gave her new insight into their meaning. When we read the words "our sins," we automatically think this means only the sins we have committed. But He revealed to her that we all carry more on ourselves than just the sins *we* have committed. We also carry on ourselves, weighing us down, all the sins that have been committed *against* us. This brings a whole new light to this scripture of promise.

"If we confess our sins…" Those we have committed against God and others *and* those committed against us. "…He is faithful and just to forgive our sins…" meaning to pardon, absolve, and free us "…from all unrighteousness."

Wow! What a freeing revelation. But God didn't stop there with Sara.

He took her to Matthew 6:14–15, which declares, "For if you forgive men when they sin against you, your heavenly Father will also forgive you. But if you do not forgive men their sins against you, your Father will not forgive your sins." Meaning, that if He is willing to extend His full grace and forgiveness to us, for all the sins we've committed—no matter the sins—we must likewise be willing and proactive to extend the same grace and forgiveness to all those who have sinned against us, no matter their sins. Without this grace and forgiveness toward ourselves and others, as He graciously offers each of us without condition, His death on the cross for the sins of all mankind is meaningless.

God is no respecter of persons. He clearly states in Acts 10:34–35, "God does not show favoritism but accepts men from every nation who fear him and do what is right." God sees *all* sin as equal, and *all* men as equal sinners. "For all have sinned and fall short of the glory of God" (Romans 3:23).

He revealed to Sara in Matthew 18:35 with what attitude we are to forgive others—"...forgive your brother from the heart," meaning sincere, heartfelt forgiveness, not lip service.

Whoa! Sara had a whole lifetime of sins committed against her—wretched sins that provoked, fueled, and festered in her deep wrath, all-consuming hatred, and near mortal injury. Sins that had left her emotionally and spiritually crippled, hindering her from being all she knew inside she had the potential to be, and God was asking her to extend His grace and forgiveness to her dad, and to do so with sincerity of heart. Not for her dad, but toward her own, complete freedom.

How can I possibly forgive him for all the evil he has done against me, and the destruction he has inflicted in my life that I am still struggling to overcome? And how can I possibly forgive him sincerely from my heart?

Sara realized how utterly impossible this would be on her own, but she trusted God, His Word, and His faithfulness, therefore she trusted what He was asking of her. Again, it had come down to a simple matter of choice—a change of mindset.

In order to truly, sincerely forgive her dad from her heart, she would have to consciously choose to begin thinking differently, against the way she naturally thought about her dad. It was a choice—her choice. Forgiving her dad would not be for his benefit; it would be for her own—for *her* freedom. It would not be about him. It was easier to hang on to the habit of resentment and hatred, and the desire for revenge; but would she choose her own desires or the freedom of heart and mind that comes from following the principles of God's Word? She chose God, again.

She began to make a daily—sometimes hourly—choice to practice forgiving her dad until it became a true sincerity of heart. It was a *process*, as forgiveness often is. But she could only make this progression, this monumental change of heart and mind that would free her more, by changing her mindset daily to think as God thinks, not as she would naturally think, proving Romans 12:2, "…be transformed by the renewing of your mind." Sara could truly be changed. She could be *transformed* by *renewing* her mind—her thought processes.

Along the way, Sara began to understand that to forgive her dad sincerely from her heart did *not* mean that she would be condoning the sins he had committed against her. It did *not* mean that she would be negating or denying the relevance of those sins against her, or the evidence and truth of those sins. It simply meant that she would completely appeal to and rely on God's supernatural power and divine example to extend His mercy, grace, and forgiveness by the renewing of her mind, her heart, and her attitude, so she would be free.

The journey toward sincere forgiveness for deeply hurtful acts is seldom an easy one, but one Sara chose because her *real* "daddy"—her "Abba, Father"—asked this of her. He asks this of everyone, you and me—no matter the sins perpetrated against us—just as He is willing to forgive us our sins.

"And forgive us our debts, as we forgive our debtors" (Matthew 6:12). Our debts are our sins. "And lead us not into temptation…" To get revenge or to harbor bitterness. "…but deliver us from evil."

Was it easy for Sara to forgive? No way—not at all. It

was an arduous, daily journey of choice and mindset, just as anything valuable in life, worth gain, is not easy.

By forgiving her dad sincerely from her heart, she would gain a whole new level of freedom. Again, it was *not* about her dad; it was about her own freedom and healing. She would be released from the cancerous emotions holding her in bondage—deep rage, bitterness, resentment, and hatred. What's more, sincere forgiveness would allow her to better know the depths of God's love for *all* mankind—both the victims *and* the villains. It would develop in her a greater testimony to others of His promises and His characteristics of unconditional love, mercy, grace, and forgiveness toward all—every person.

Everything comes back to a *choice.*

There is a choice in everything we face in life, from the most inconsequential, day-to-day things to the most significant life-altering things. As a mentally capable adult, no other person has the authority or right to make a choice for you. Your choices are your own. Others can advise and persuade, they can manipulate and bully, but the power of choice belongs to you alone. With this in mind, we must realize that we each have the choice to serve God or Satan, God or man. There is *no* gray area, *no* in-between, *no* sitting on the fence. "He who is not with me is against me" (Matthew 12:30).

When Sara began to choose to practice forgiveness—for the benefit of her own freedom—she began to choose a life that was no longer about her suffering and surviving. It was no longer about her debilitations and defeat. It was no longer about self-pity and self-abhorrence. It was about her being daily transformed by the renewing of her mind toward becoming *all* that God had created and purposed her to be from before the foundation of time. It was about *thriving*.

> "Do not conform any longer to the pattern of this world, but be transformed by the renewing of your mind. Then you will be able to test and approve what God's will is—his good, pleasing and perfect will" (Romans 12:2, NIV).
>
> "...the pattern of this world..." is to hold on to the sins committed against us—the hatred, the anger, the injustice, the revenge. But "...the renewing of your mind..." is to work daily at changing the way you naturally want to think, to the way God thinks. How do we know how God thinks? He is an open Book. He is the Word of God, the Living Word, revealing all that He is and all that He desires for you.

Sara, the tender growing flower, had finally burst through the dark and oppressive soil and into the bright and freeing light of day when she was truly able to say from a sincere heart for the first time, *I forgive my dad*. It was not for him that she had taken this journey; it was for herself.

Was everything all wonderful and bright then? No, *no*. She learned that she would be forgiving her dad over and over again, sometimes monthly, sometimes daily—continually renewing her mind. She learned that sin and evil is persistent. It requires the full armor of God to stand against and defeat:

Finally, be strong in the Lord and in his mighty power. Put on the full armor of God so that you can take your stand against the devil's schemes. For our struggle is not against flesh and blood, but against the rulers, against the authorities, against the powers of this dark world and against the spiritual forces of evil in the heavenly realms. Therefore put on the full armor of God, so that when the day of evil comes, you may be able to stand your ground, and after you have done everything, to stand. Stand firm then, with the belt of truth buckled around your waist, with the breastplate of righteousness in place, and with your feet fitted with the readiness that comes from the gospel of peace. In addition to all this, take up the shield of faith, with which you can extinguish all the flaming arrows of the evil one. Take the helmet of salvation and the sword of the Spirit, which is the word of God. And pray in the Spirit on all occasions with all kinds of prayers and requests. With this in mind, be alert and always keep on praying for all the saints.

Ephesians 6:10–18

Sara learned that forgiveness is often a process, but that forgiveness of even your worst enemy *is very possible* because "with God, all things are possible" (Matthew 19:26).

Chapter Twenty-Two

Early in her marriage to Greg and long before she came to the place of forgiving her dad, Sara boldly chose to reestablish a relationship with her mother and brothers that her dad had severed ten years prior. He had stolen something else very precious from her that she was now determined to take back—her family. She was learning that she had the power and authority to make those choices, simply because she was an individual, a grown up with a fully functioning, capable mind. She was taking back her power, taking back her freedom of choice by walking back into her family's lives with her head held high. Not from an arrogant pride, but from a deep confidence and understanding of what was right and just and true, and from knowing who she was as a human being and child of God. She was an individual created by the living God who had uniquely formed her and destined her for a specific purpose in life, just as He had created every human being. It was time for a new mindset—to take back the dignity and wholesome pride that her dad had stolen from her long before and to take back her family.

Sara had no desire, whatsoever, to see her dad—and forgiveness did not necessitate she resume a relationship with him. Renewing a relationship with those she loved had nothing to do with him. Her coming back into his life to reconnect with her mother and siblings wasn't about him; it was about those she loved and desired to spend quality time with: her mother, Allie, Matt, John, and Wayne.

Seeing her dad and being around him in the mix was a small price to pay when the family all gathered for the long Thanksgiving weekend each year. For three to four days, her sister and brothers and their families would gather at their parents' house—the house she had been raised in, where so many horrors had taken place. It was difficult, yes, to walk back into that house for the first time after so many years. It was difficult, yes, to walk back into the presence of her dad after so long, but she was determined to be *all* that God had created her to be, and to honor who He was, by never again allowing another human being to rob her of the treasures He had purposed for her—free will, dignity, self-worth, choices.

Each Thanksgiving, as Sara reentered her old neighborhood and her childhood home came into view, her armor of protection would rise like a steel shield about her. She'd take on different characteristics than Greg and their son, Scott, knew. She transformed from a gentle, caring woman to a harder, louder, less tolerant one. It was a natural defense, a survival response that would emerge in order for her be able to walk back into that house—head high—stand strong in the face of her dad, and be around him in that house, for three to four days straight.

Sara and her dad were polite to each other. That was the extent of their relationship, and rightly so. What little conversation they had was limited, by Sara's choice, to inconsequential things. However, what was not at all inconsequential was the *huge lie* that stood hefty and mountainous between them. When Sara reentered her childhood home for the first time, in the face of all the things that had transpired since her birth, she had to make room for the pyramid of pretense that filled the atmosphere because of all the years of abuse that were never spoken of. No one was going to talk about the past. Her dad was not going to humble himself and own up to his responsibility of abuse and ill behaviors of his own accord. It had all been quietly and purposefully padlocked in the chest of disregard. No one wanted to open that old, screeching lid and let demons fly—not even Sara. She wasn't *that* brave—yet. No one wanted to cause anyone to feel more uncomfortable than they did already, and had for years. After all, it was old news, right? What was past was past, right? Everyone had *survived* and gotten on with living, right? *Wrong.* Everyone may have gotten on with living—and Sara *had* sincerely forgiven him in her heart, for herself—but she was not living in complete wholeness, truth, or freedom yet.

Pretense is defined as, "A false showing of something." Pretense is wrong and it breeds sin and evil. This huge lie, this pretense that stood between them—like a huge, graven idol they bowed to out of fear—was another great bondage in Sara's life that God revealed to her. A bondage He wanted her to be freed from. His divine purpose for her was to be completely whole and free, unencumbered by *any* bondage. This pretense between them was indeed a bondage to sin. Not one that Sara had created, but a bondage she was choosing by allowing the pretense to continue. As an adult, she had the power to choose right or wrong, good or evil, God or Satan, God or man. By keeping the padlock on the chest of disregard, she was choosing to condone all the sins her dad had chosen to commit against her by not speaking the truth of those sins, and how they had grossly shaped and adversely affected her life. By her silence, she was choosing to allow him freedom from just accountability and consequences, thus keeping herself in bondage. It was simply wrong—for her.

Early in her first marriage, to Ted, she had telephoned her dad and made a restrained and insecure attempt to confront him about the abuses and ill-behaviors she'd suffered at his hands throughout her childhood. He chose to respond in defense, making excuses and actually attempting to put the blame on her instead of taking his rightful ownership. He was the adult, she had been the child. He had made conscious, wicked, repulsive, immoral, merciless adult choices against his daughter and his other children that had crippled her in multiple ways for many years to follow. The right thing, the just thing, the Godly thing, if he was truly a child of God, would have been for him to take responsibility for his adult choices and confess his misdeeds with sincere regret and humility. Everything comes back to choices.

Years later, after she had married Greg, and she had grown more fully into the confidence of who she was in

Christ, the Lord began working in her heart again, this time about her willingness to walk out Matthew 18. By removing the padlock from that ancient chest of disregard, exposing the lie—the pretense between them—Sara would gain an even greater freedom of heart and mind that would allow her to become even more the woman God was growing and stretching her to be. "If your brother sins against you, go and show him his fault, just between the two of you. If he listens to you, you have won your brother over" (Matthew 18:15).

Her dad professed to be saved—a child of God—a Christian. As long as Sara could remember, her dad had proclaimed to be a man of God. By theological and Biblical definition, he was therefore her spiritual brother—though contrary to his behaviors. Because he professed salvation—Christianity—it was Sara's spiritual, Biblical obligation by God's principles to seek him out and show him his faults against her. But it would be her choice alone to take that courageous step a second time.

In October 1996, after much prayerful consideration and preparation, Sara took the courageous steps to walk out Matthew 18 in faith, believing God's promise that He would work this for her good.

The choice she made to do the right and just thing by confronting him was a very difficult one, as you can imagine. But she was compelled to choose God's ways and follow His direction all the way. Her entire life had necessitated faith and trust in God. She was learning that He always had her best interest at heart, and that her obedience to Him was necessary to achieve and acquire the best He had for her spiritually, mentally, emotionally, and physically. Obedience to her true Daddy—her heavenly Father—was essential to bringing about His promise of abundant life. This particular situation—obeying God's directive to confront her dad—would bring about the promise of Romans 8:28, "…in all things God works for the good of those who love him, who have been called according to his purpose."

Sara loved God; therefore, His promise was to work *all* things for her good. She had to believe that confronting her dad would result in her good. She knew that she was "called according to His purpose," because she had sincerely accepted Jesus as her Savior and firmly believed, based on scripture, that she would never lose her salvation. "For God so loved the world that he gave his one and only Son, that whoever believes in him shall not perish but have eternal life" (John 3:16).

Prayer of Psalm 119:41–47
May your unfailing love come to me, O LORD,
your salvation according to your promise;
then I will answer the one who taunts me,
for I trust in your word.
Do not snatch the word of truth from my mouth,
for I have put my hope in your laws.
I will always obey your law,
for ever and ever.
I will walk about in freedom,
for I have sought out your precepts.
I will speak of your statutes before kings
and will not be put to shame,
for I delight in your commands…
because I love them.

Because Sara's actions would directly affect her siblings and the family's future gatherings and dynamics, she telephoned each of them and shared her and Greg's decision to follow Matthew 18. Allie, Matt, John, and Wayne each responded with 100% support and encouragement, knowing that Sara and Greg's decision was the right choice, necessary for Sara's further healing and freedom from her past.

She presented to her dad every issue of abuse she had suffered at his hands, and how the abuses had affected her life. She unlocked the rusty chest, freed all the ugly, rotting contents, and shed the light of truth on every issue, covering all the years she had spent under his evil authority. Her hope, her prayer, was that he would fully acknowledge them all this time, own up to every account, take responsibility for his adult choices, and truly, sincerely be repentant.

Separately, Greg took the same step. He shared with Sara's dad, from his perspective as her husband, how the abuses had affected him in their marriage. And he expressed how he saw Sara change each time they all gathered for the Thanksgiving weekend.

Neither she nor Greg had any idea how her dad might respond. It was truly an act of faith and obedience to God. They knew that speaking the truth, destroying the pretense, would resonate throughout Sara's family, to her mother, her sister and brothers, and their families. Most drastically, it would affect her mother, whom Sara loved with all her heart and never wanted to unnecessarily hurt. But her mother had made her own adult choices, and this was not about her mother, either. It was not about her dad, her mother, her sister, or her brothers. It was about Sara's own, personal, further healing and freedom. She

JEN MILLER

had needed to confront her dad for herself—and because it was the right and just thing by God's principles.

This paramount act of faith forced another question—how would she and Greg choose to respond to Sara's dad should he once again choose to deny his responsibility of sins against her? The right choice for every circumstance under the sun can be found in God's life-giving Word. So, Sara and her husband explored further the instructions of Matthew 18:16–17. "But if he will not listen, take one or two others along, so that every matter may be established by the testimony of two or three witnesses. If he refuses to listen to them, tell it to the church; and if he refuses to listen even to the church, treat him as you would a pagan or a tax collector."

Should Sara's dad choose to ignore the truths she and Greg presented, the next steps were clearly laid out for them. Ultimately, his ignoring the truth would mean there would be no more relationship with him. Should her mother continue to choose allegiance with him in that circumstance, there would be no further relationship with her, except apart from him. Sara and Greg had to be mentally and emotionally prepared for these possibilities. It was a very difficult decision to risk losing her mother all over again. But that would be a choice her mother alone would have to make. Whatever the outcome, Sara and Greg had made the choice to commit it all to God, trusting that He would indeed work *all* things for their good because they loved Him and were called according to His purpose—no matter her dad's or her mother's decisions.

Amazing to Sara and Greg was the response they got from Sara's dad. On that particular day of reckoning, he appeared to be a sincerely broken and repentant man—before God, Sara, and Greg. He acknowledged to Sara, and owned up to, every act of abuse, neglect, and ill behavior that she had confronted him with. He gave no excuses and brought no defense. He shared that he had asked God to forgive him, and he hoped that Sara and Greg might someday forgive him as well, if they could possibly ever find it in their hearts to do so. Sara already had…long before she had taken the steps to follow Matthew 18.

There were still questions remaining that may never be answered in this lifetime. If he had truly been repentant of his gross misdeeds, which encompassed conscious choices of sin and evil over the span of nineteen years, why had he never *voluntarily* owned up to Sara? Why had it taken the prompting by Sara's confrontation a *second* time? The first time she had confronted him, in her early twenties, during her first marriage, he had taken *no* responsibility for his blatant sins against her, and had even blamed *her* for his evil actions. If he had sincerely had a change of heart, through true repentance, since that first confrontation, would the change of heart not have prompted a new attitude with different thinking? Would he not have been compelled to step up and take responsibility, of his *own* volition—instead of only when Sara had confronted him a second time, years later? And, if he had *truly, sincerely* been repentant, why had she and her siblings seen no real changes in his character since—his actions, reactions, and interactions toward them or their mother?

Only God knows the heart of man. It was not for Sara, Greg, or her siblings to judge. Judgment of Sara's dad was God's divine responsibility. Only her dad, and God, knows the real truths of his heart. Sara's only responsibility and authority was in confronting him out of her own personal need to speak the truth, hear him take responsibility, and ask her for forgiveness, without excuses or defense.

God is no respecter of persons. He is in the business of transforming *all* lives, those of the victims *and* the villains who are willing and truly sincere. "He is patient with you, not wanting anyone to perish, but everyone to come to repentance" (2 Peter 3:9).

God loves *all* mankind, despite their choices toward sin and evil. He longs for every person to come to Him in repentance and faith—the victims *and* the villains.

All women and men are victims of the devastation of sin, and all are villains from time to time. "There is no one righteous, not even one" (Romans 3:10). No one is without blame; therefore every man, woman, and child needs salvation and redemption that can only come through God's loving, gracious forgiveness through His Son, Jesus. It's a sincere, personal choice that every human has been granted.

> True repentance will bring about true change, and a desire to pro-actively pursue change. As a forgiven child of God, we will then have a desire to strive toward exemplifying God's characteristics, and we will bare the fruit of the Spirit in our daily life which is "love, joy, peace, patience, kindness, goodness, faithfulness, gentleness and self-control.

Against such things there is no law. Those who belong to Christ Jesus have crucified the sinful nature with its passions and desires. Since we live by the Spirit, let us keep in step with the Spirit. Let us not become conceited, provoking and envying each other" (Galatians 5:22-26).

What was critical for Sara was her own further healing, in part achieved by confronting her abuser. Further healing was in hearing him take responsibility and own up to every inexcusable act she had confronted him with. She was made more free and whole because *she* had made a choice to take the courageous step to stand up and speak the truth against sin and evil.

Do Sara and her dad have a close relationship today? No ... no. But there is no longer a falsehood lingering in the air. The truth has been spoken. Does Sara still struggle with being in that house each Thanksgiving that she chooses to participate? You bet! Every room that she enters throughout those three days is a constant reminder of the horrors, but she has changed and knows that God has given her more than enough grace to be *all* she was created to be, even in the midst of those reminders. That is His glory and power revealed through obedience to His Word.

Along the journey toward becoming all that God had created and purposed her to be, Sara began to truly see and understand that when she was thirteen years old and asked God to forgive her sins and be her Savior; she was adopted at that very moment into the Kingdom of God. She instantly became an *heir* to the throne of God, making her a daughter of the King of Kings—a princess. Not by any good deeds or penitence she had done. Salvation is a *free* gift from God to *all* who choose to accept it from a humble and sincere heart of faith—victim or villain. She had been a villain from time to time herself, and most definitely a straying child of God, not unlike the prodigal son exampled in Luke 15—but no less God's daughter, forgiven, cleansed, redeemed, and being transformed daily into His likeness.

> The Apostle Paul teaches us in Gal 4:4-7 that, "…God sent his Son… to redeem those under law, that we might receive the full rights of sons (and daughters). Because you are sons [daughters], God sent the Spirit of his Son into our hearts, the Spirit who calls out, "Abba, Father." (Meaning 'Daddy'.) So you are no longer a slave, but a son [daughter]; and since you are a son [daughter], God has made you also an heir.

Sara began to see that although she is in human form with a sin nature, God sees her as His princess, clothed in righteousness, with all her sins covered by the blood of Jesus. Sara had had a faithful and true Daddy all along—her Abba, heavenly Father. He never left her and never would. He had always loved her without condition, held her close, comforted her, carried her—and always would.

Chapter Twenty-Three

In the fall of 2006, as Sara was prayerfully drafting her life story to share with you, the Spirit took her to Revelation 2:17 and *knocked the breath out of her* with a profound revelation of this scripture to her own life. He promises,

> *To him who overcomes,*
> *I will give some of the hidden manna.*
> *I will also give him a white stone*
> *with a new name written on it,*
> *known only to him who receives it.*

He revealed to Sara how each of these promises had already been amazingly and profoundly fulfilled in her life.

"To him who overcomes, I will give some of the hidden manna…" It was the hidden manna of God (His Word), that fed and nurtured Sara's spirit throughout her life, giving her the strength and courage to keep going, to keep hoping, to keep praying, to choose life, and to choose faith and hope in God.

"… I will also give him a … new name … known only to him who receives it." The promise of a new name given to those who overcome has been most stunningly fulfilled in Sara's life. You see, the name Sara is not the name my friend was given at birth by her parents. She's a writer, and sometime during our early thirties she began penning her work as Sara. I know it's not uncommon for writers to have a ghost name they use to write under, so I didn't think much of it, though I was curious as to why the name Sara. I finally asked her one day, "Why the name Sara? What made you choose that name?"

She stopped at the question, an introspective look coming to her face. She had never before considered this question. She was lost within herself for a few minutes then shared with me that for years she had felt very drawn to that name, as if it were her true name—the name she was really meant to have. She said that it felt right and warm and comfortable, safe, and pure, and that deep inside she felt like the name truly belonged to her. So, when the Spirit took her to Revelation 2:17, which promises a new name to him who overcomes, it stunned her to realize that the name she had known in her heart for so many years, was the name God had given her—Sara.

It was then that she looked up the meaning of the name Sara, and what she uncovered stunned her even more as to how intimately God loves and works within each and every one of us, and has detailed *every* minute aspect of our lives … right down to our name and the significance of its meaning. He's even numbered the very hairs of our head, declares Matthew 10:30, "And even the very hairs of your head are all numbered." Amazing!

In Jeremiah 1:5, He shares just how intimately He knows us and loves us. "Before I formed you in the womb I knew you, before you were born I set you apart."

Wow…how can you doubt His love for you? And with such a profound love and intimacy for you, there must also be a purpose for your life.

The name Sara is from Hebrew origin. The spiritual connotation is *beloved*. Its inherent meaning is *princess*. You see, Sara's true Daddy, her Abba, Father, not only *calls* her a princess because she is an heir to His throne—not unlike many loving, earthly daddies call their daughters—but Sara's true Father went a step further in His promise to reward her for overcoming— He *named* her princess! That's how good and faithful God is to us, no matter how we have suffered or sinned.

"…I will also give him a white stone with a new name written on it…" The significance of the white stone is incredibly profound to Sara's life as well. Her birthstone, being born on Father's Day in June, is a beautiful white stone—a pearl. What makes this white stone so profound to Sara's life is the process by which a pearl is formed.

Sara has framed in her home a powerful excerpt from Pastor Charles Swindoll's book, *Growing Strong in the Seasons of Life*. What he wrote so exactly exemplifies Sara's life and purpose that she often reads it and weeps, not in sorrow, but in amazement, joy, and gladness as Isaiah 61:3 promises, "…the oil of joy for mourning, and a garment of praise for the spirit of despair."

As you read the excerpt, I believe you will be just as amazed to see all the parallels and symbolisms so significant to Sara's life.

Pearls

Pearls are the product of pain. For some unknown reason, the shell of the oyster gets pierced and an alien substance—a grain of sand—slips inside. On the entry of that foreign irritant, all the resources within the tiny, sensitive oyster rush to the spot and begin to release healing fluids that otherwise would have remained dormant. By and by the irritant is covered and the wound is healed—by a *pearl*.

No other gem has so fascinating a history. It is the symbol of stress—a healed wound...a precious, tiny jewel conceived through irritation, born of adversity, nursed by adjustments. Had there been no wounding, no irritating interruption, there could have been no pearl. Some oysters are never wounded...and those who seek for gems toss them aside, fit only for stew.

No wonder our heavenly home has as its entrance *pearly* gates! Those who go through them need no explanation. They are the ones who have been wounded, bruised, and have responded to the sting of irritations with the pearl of adjustment.[8]

Epilogue

My name is Jen, the author of this true story. But my *new* name, my God-given, spiritual name is *Sara*. You've just experienced my life journey—my autobiography—my transformation from seedling to daisy to oak, my life from surviving to *thriving*.

My life is a testimony to the fact that God *is* alive and working intimately in *each* of our lives—your life. It's a testimony to His amazing characteristics and transforming power—for you. It's a testimony that proves that His promises *are* real—for you.

I'm a living, breathing, *thriving*, real-life miracle, like many of you.

I pray that through my life story, you will better see and know, as never before, the truths and promises of these scriptures—for you.

With God all things are possible.
Matthew 19:26b (NKJV)

All things are possible to him who believes.
Mark 9:23 (NKJV)

I can do all things through Christ who strengthens me
Philippians 4:13 (NKJV)

I have overcome the evil, the ugly, the atrocities of my life by sheer hope and faith in the one, true, and living God, in companion with perserverance and hard work. I was not satisfied to remain simply a survivor, living in mediocrity day to day. *Are you?*

I wanted more, and knew I had the potential to be and to do so much more despite emotional crippling. I wanted the abundant life that Jesus promises in John 10:10 (NKJV), *Do you?*

"I have come that they may have life, and have it more abundantly."

I believed. I had hope and faith in God for a future, for His promises of freedom and joy. I overcame, and His promises were made *full* and *real* in my life, just as they can be in yours. *Do you believe?*

♥ ♥ ♥

Today, I am more than a survivor; I'm a *thriver*, as I've termed it. But, if you were to meet me today, and get to know me, what else would you find? You'd see that I'm an everyday, ordinary wife, mom, sister, daughter, aunt, friend ... and you'd find that I'm also still a sinner. I'm human and therefore still live with a sin nature—a tendency toward thinking and acting on that which is not right or just. It's *still* a daily choice for me to be transformed by the renewing of my mind.

Like each and every one of us, I disappoint people and let them down. I don't always think the right thoughts or say the right things. I don't always do the right things or make the best choices. I'm not always the best mom, wife, friend…Life is still a struggle, like yours, because we're still living with a sin nature. *But here is the difference*, knowing God intimately, having a personal relationship with Him through Jesus Christ that results in knowing who we are in Christ. This gives us a foundational confidence that we would otherwise not have. It gives us courage and strength to meet each new day, no matter the circumstances, with hope and faith—and perseverance. It gives us the confidence to become *all* that God has created us to be.

Today, I truly know who I am—a child of God, His daughter, His beloved, His princess, an heir to His throne, covered by the blood of Jesus, cleansed, white, whole and…*free.*

If God will forgive and free me from my multitude of sins and from all the sins committed against me, He will most surely free you from all that you carry. He will lift you up from the mire of sin and evil and set your feet on the Rock—just like He has for me.

> *I waited patiently for the LORD;*
> *he turned to me and heard my cry.*
> *He lifted me out of the slimy pit,*
> *out of the mud and mire;*
> *He set my feet on a rock*

> *and gave me a firm place to stand.*
> *He put a new song in my mouth,*
> *a hymn of praise to our God.*
> *Many will see and fear*
> *and put their trust in the* LORD.

Psalm 40:1–3

Today, if I were to recite my childhood prayer, it would go like this: "Now I lay me down to sleep. I praise you, God, for Your great peace. If I should die before I wake, I thank You, Abba, I'll see Your face."

❤ ❤ ❤

Your loving, gracious, freeing God is right there with you now, as you are reading this. He is longing for you to come to Him, simply and humbly through prayer, to tell Him all that is on your heart. He already knows, He knows you well, He created you, but He wants a relationship with you—a dialogue. Like a truly loving, caring, protective dad would want to hear from his grown daughter, his son, and be an intricate part of your life, so much more God wants you to seek Him out, talk with Him—share all of your life with Him. He wants to give you true freedom, abiding joy, and everlasting peace that results from knowing and loving Him daily, which will carry you through all the challenges and tragedies and beauty of life, and carry you into eternity under the sheltering wings of His glorious presence.

If you haven't already talked with Him and confessed all the sins you carry—those you've committed *and* those committed against you—tell Him right now, just as you are. With

NOW I LAY ME DOWN TO SLEEP: THE STORY OF SARA

a sincere and humble heart, ask Him to forgive your sins—to free you once and for all, for all of eternity. Don't put this life-changing *choice* off another second, for He declares that, "…now is the time of God's favor, now is the day of salvation" (2 Corinthians 6:2).

Coming to Him in prayer with a sincere heart is a simple act of faith that He will do what He promises, "If we confess our sins, he is faithful and just and will forgive us our sins and purify us from all unrighteousness" (1 John 1:9).

Simply talk to Him now, using the following prayer from a sincere heart, and you will forever be His child, an heir to the throne of God, with *all* His promises laid at your feet like treasure. All that He has is yours—right now. He only asks that you simply trust Him and obey His Word. Pray with me now in faith, believing; then write to me so I can share in your life-changing choice:

Oh, God, I know I am a sinner.
I know that I do not deserve your forgiveness.
Cleanse me now from all the sins
I have committed against you and against others.
Cleanse me now from all the sins
that have been committed against me,
so that I might truly be set free.

Give me the grace to forgive others from my heart,
just as you are forgiving me.
Place your Spirit to live inside me
and help me to see myself as you now see me—
whole and clean and forgiven from this moment on,
your daughter, your son, an heir to your throne.

> *Teach me to love myself and others as you love me.*
> *In the name of Jesus I ask all these things,*
> *and I thank you, Abba, Father. Amen.*

If you talked with God sincerely through this prayer today or in sincere prayer at some earlier time in your life, asking Him to forgive you and be your Savior, God sees you as beautiful and transformed, whole and renewed. *How do you see yourself?*

Do you see yourself the way God truly sees you? Or do you still believe the lies? Do you love yourself and treat yourself as the beautiful creation God has nurtured and wept over, and as an heir to all that He is and all that He has? If not, "Be transformed by the renewing of your mind" (Romans 12:2). It's your choice—a daily choice to work at changing the way you naturally want to think about yourself, to the way God thinks about you.

Begin today.

This is the greatest miracle of all—God's redemptive power, transforming us daily into His likeness, His characteristics, if we have accepted Jesus into our hearts, *no matter how we've suffered or sinned.*

The sun retires beneath a
blanket of silver splashed blackness
As warm summer breezes gently close rose petals
And bid the birds goodnight.

The moon smiles and ...
"Now I lay me down to sleep"
as dew falls softly
cooling the earth and air.

The world grows quiet ...
Taken up in dreams and fantasies
Harmonized by the cricket's song.

–Jen Miller, aka "Sara"

♥ ♥ ♥

Now, my friend, I encourage you to take the next step toward becoming *all* that God has divinely created you to be—*more* than a survivor of the things life throws your way—a *thriver*!

I encourage you to get a copy of the powerful study, *Becoming All God Created Me To Be*, co-authored by The Sara Ministry team and myself for *every* woman and man. Please visit our web site today at www.sara-ministry.com.

Are you a survivor of emotional, physical, and/or sexual child-hood abuse? I encourage you to get a copy of our powerful recovery study, *Thrivers*, co-authored by Amber Reatherford and myself. It will change your life! Visit our web site today.

> *The Lord bless you and keep you;*
> *the Lord make his face shine upon you*
> *and be gracious to you;*
> *the Lord turn his face toward you*
> *and give you peace.*
> Amen.
> Number 6:24

Are you a "covert" abuser? Do you verbally,
physically, and/or sexually harm yourself?

Are you an "overt" abuser? Do you verbally,
physically, and/or sexually harm others?

Abusers become abusers by no fault of their own.
Abusers stay abusers by choice.

It's your choice.
Pick up the phone and get help—now.
It's readily available to you.
Open your phone book to Psychologists
and find one who practices Godly principles.
There are no excuses.
Make the call now.

"I tell you, now is the time of God's favor, now is the
day of salvation."
"... and the truth will make you free."

2 Corinthians 6:2 and John 8:32 (KJV)

Sara's life story has inspired women and men of all back-
grounds to no longer be satisfied with simply surviving day-
to-day life. It has fueled the desire to become all God created
them to be. As a result, *Becoming ALL God Created Me To Be*
was written by Jen Miller and team members of The Sara
Ministry Foundation. This powerful study, as well as *Thrivers*

and other invaluable studies and books, is available through The Sara Ministry Foundation for both individual and small group study. Please visit us at www.sara-ministry.com.

You may correspond with Jen Miller and other authors of The Sara Ministry Foundation through our web site. We hope to hear from you.

Notes

1 *Fight or Flight* is our body's primitive, automatic, inborn response to attack, harm or threat to our survival that prepares the body to "fight" or "flee." When this response is activated, our body undergoes a series of very dramatic changes physically and psychologically in an effort of survival.

The evidence is overwhelming that there is a cumulative buildup of stress hormones. If not properly metabolized over time, the excessive stress can lead to disorders of our nervous system, hormonal and immune systems. *Mind / Body Education Center Online*, "The Fight or Flight Response," http://www.thebodysoulconnection.com/EducationCenter/fkight.html (accessed November 1, 2007).

2 *Body memory* is the theory that the body itself is capable

of storing memories, as opposed to only the brain. This is used to explain having memories for events where the brain was not in a position to store memories (dissociation), and is sometimes a catalyst for repressed memories recovery. These memories are often characterized with phantom pain in a part or parts of the body—the body appearing to remember the past trauma.

In order to gain a body memory, according to the theory, one needs to go through a traumatic experience and the body may store this memory in any place in the body that participated in the event—such as the arm, if it got burnt.

Symptoms: Recurrent behavior patterns, flashbacks, emotional responses, pain, or other sensations, generally associated with certain triggers (memories, events, people, colors, sounds, skin pressure, etc). *Wikipedia Online,* s.v. "Body Memory," http://en.wikipedia.org/wiki/Body_memory (accessed November 1, 2007).

3 *Dissociation* is a mental process, which produces a lack of connection in a person's thoughts, memories, feelings, actions, or sense of identity. During the period of time when a person is dissociating, certain information is not associated with other information as it normally would be. For example, during a traumatic experience, a person may dissociate the memory of the place and circumstances of the trauma from his ongoing memory, resulting in a temporary mental escape from the fear and pain of the trauma and, in some cases, a memory gap surrounding the experience. Because this process can produce changes in memory, people who frequently

dissociate often find their senses of personal history and identity are affected.

Most clinicians believe that dissociation exists on a continuum of severity. This continuum reflects a wide range of experiences and/or symptoms. At one end are mild dissociative experiences common to most people, such as daydreaming, highway hypnosis, or "getting lost" in a book or movie, all of which involve "losing touch" with conscious awareness of one's immediate surroundings. At the other extreme is complex, chronic dissociation, resulting in serious impairment or inability to function.

When faced with overwhelmingly traumatic situations from which there is no physical escape, a child may resort to "going away" in his or her head. Children typically use this ability as an extremely effective defense against acute physical and emotional pain, or anxious anticipation of that pain. By this dissociative process, thoughts, feelings, memories, and perceptions of the traumatic experiences can be separated off psychologically, allowing the child to function as if the trauma had not occurred.

Dissociation is often referred to as a highly creative survival technique because it allows individuals enduring "hopeless" circumstances to preserve some areas of healthy functioning. Over time, however, for a child who has been repeatedly physically and sexually assaulted, defensive dissociation becomes reinforced and conditioned. Because the dissociative escape is so effective, children who are very practiced at it may automatically use it whenever they feel threatened or anxious—even if the anxiety-producing situation is not extreme or abusive.

Repeated dissociation may result in a series of separate entities, or mental states, which may eventually take on identities of their own, called multiple personalities.

Some people with Dissociative Disorders have a tendency toward self-persecution, self-sabotage, and even violence (both self-inflicted and/or outwardly directed). The vast majority (as many as 98 to 99%) of individuals who develop Dissociative Disorders have documented histories of repetitive, overwhelming, and often life-threatening trauma at a sensitive developmental stage of childhood (usually before the age of nine). In our culture the most frequent precursor to Dissociative Disorders is extreme physical, emotional, and sexual abuse in childhood, but survivors of other kinds of trauma in childhood (such as natural disasters, invasive medical procedures, war, kidnapping, and torture) have also reacted by developing Dissociative Disorders.

Sidran Institute–Tramatic Stress Education & Advocacy Online, "What Is Dissociation?" http://www.sidran.org/sub.cfm?contentID=75&sectionid=4 (accessed November 1, 2007).

4 *Self-injury (SI)*—also known as self-harm or self-mutilation—is defined as any intentional injury to one's own body. It usually either leaves marks or causes tissue damage. It is hard for most people to understand why someone would want to cut or burn himself/herself. The mere idea of intentionally inflicting wounds to oneself makes people cringe. Yet there are growing numbers of young people who do intentionally hurt themselves. Understanding the phenomenon is the first step in changing it.

There is no simple portrait of a person who intentionally

injures him/herself. This behavior is not limited by gender, race, education, age, sexual orientation, socio-economics, or religion. However, there are some commonly seen factors:

- *Self-injury more commonly occurs in adolescent females.*
- *Many self-injurers have a history of physical, emotional or sexual abuse.*
- *Many self-injurers have co-existing problems of substance abuse, obsessive-compulsive disorder (or compulsive alone), or eating disorders.*
- *Self-injuring individuals were often raised in families that discouraged expression of anger, and tend to lack skills to express their emotions.*
- *Self-injurers often lack a good social support network.*

The most common ways that people self-injure are:

- *Cutting*
- *Burning (or "branding" with hot objects)*
- *Picking at skin or re-opening wounds*
- *Hair-pulling (trichotillomania)*
- *Hitting (with hammer or other object)*
- *Bone-breaking*
- *Head-banging (more often seen in autistic, severely retarded or psychotic people)*
- *Multiple piercing or multiple tattooing*

Jaffe, Jaelline, Ph.D, and Jeanne Segal, Ph.D., Helpguide Online, "Self-Injury," http://www.helpguide.org/mental/self_injury.htm (accessed November 1, 2007).

5 *Astral Projection* is "an interpretation of out-of-body experiences (OBEs) achieved either awake or via lucid dreaming, deep meditation, or the use of psychotropics. People who say they experience astral projection often say that their consciousness or soul has transferred into an astral body (or "double"), which moves in tandem with the physical body in a "parallel world" known as the astral plane. The concept of astral projection has been around for thousands of years, dating back to ancient China. It is currently often associated with the New Age movement." *Wikipedia Online,* s.v. "Astral Projection," *Crystalinks Online,* s.v. "Astral Projection," http://www.crystalinks.com/astralprojection.html (accessed November 1, 2007)

6 *Flashback* is a psychological phenomenon in which an individual has a sudden, usually vivid, recollection of a past experience. The term is used particularly when the memory is recalled involuntarily, and/or when it is so intense that the person "relives" the experience, unable to fully recognize it as memory and not something that is happening in "real time". The medical term for the phenomenon is hypnagogic regression. *Wikipedia Online,* s.v. "Flashback" http://en.wikipedia.org/wiki/Flashback_(psychological_phenomenon) (accessed November 1, 2007).

7 *Manifestation of the Spirit.* "Now to each one the manifestation of the Spirit is given for the common good. To one there is given through the Spirit the message of wisdom, to another the message of knowledge by means of the same Spirit, to another faith by the same Spirit, to another gifts of

healing by that one Spirit, to another miraculous powers, to another prophecy, to another distinguishing between spirits, to another speaking in different kinds of tongues, and to still another the interpretation of tongues. All these are the work of one and the same Spirit, and he gives them to each one, just as he determines" (1 Corinthians 12:7–11).

8 "Pearls" taken from *Growing Strong in the Seasons of Life* by Charles R. Swindoll. (Zondervan, Grand Rapids, MI, 1994).